Markers V

Journal of the Association for Gravestone Studies

Edited by
Theodore Chase

UNIVERSITY
PRESS OF
AMERICA

BOWLING GREEN STATE
UNIVERSITY LIBRARIES

LANHAM • NEW YORK • LONDON

Copyright © 1988 by

University Press of America,® Inc.

4720 Boston Way
Lanham, MD 20706

3 Henrietta Street
London WC2E 8LU England

All rights reserved

Printed in the United States of America

British Cataloging in Publication Information Available

"Md. by Thomas Gold: The Gravestones of a New England Carver"
copyright © 1988 by Meredith M. Williams and Gray Williams, Jr.

ISBN (Perfect): 0–8191–6869–6 (pbk. : alk. paper)
ISBN (Cloth): 0–8191–6868–8 (alk. paper)
LCN: 81–642903

All University Press of America books are produced on acid-free
paper which exceeds the minimum standards set by the National
Historical Publications and Records Commission.

ASSOCIATION FOR GRAVESTONE STUDIES
EDITORIAL BOARD

Theodore Chase, Editor
David Watters, Associate Editor

John L. Brooke   James A. Slater
Jessie Lie Farber   Richard F. Welch

Manuscripts may be submitted for review to Theodore Chase, 74 Farm Street, Dover, Massachusetts 02030. Manuscripts should conform, so far as possible, to *The Chicago Manual of Style* and may be accompanied by glossy black and white photographs or black ink drawings, tables or maps. For information about other Association for Gravestone Studies publications, membership and activities, write to Rosalee Oakley, Executive Director, 46 Plymouth Road, Needham, Massachusetts 02192.

The editor wishes to thank the members of the editorial board, and particularly his predecessor, David Watters, for their advice and help in the selection and editing of articles for this edition of the journal. The editor is grateful to Carol Davidson for preparing the copy and layout.

Articles appearing in this journal are annotated and indexed in *Historical Abstracts* and *America: History and Life*.

TABLE OF CONTENTS

	Page
"Md. by Thomas Gold": The Gravestones of a New Haven Carver	1
Meredith M. Williams and Gray Williams, Jr.	
Pennsylvania German Gravestones: An Introduction	60
Thomas E. Graves	
Early Pennsylvania Gravemarkers	96
Photographs and text by Daniel and Jessie Lie Farber	
Ontario Gravestones	122
Darrell A. Norris	
Research Report on the Graveyards of Kings County, Nova Scotia	150
Deborah Trask and Debra McNabb	
Poems in Stone: The Tombs of Louis Henri Sullivan	168
Robert A. Wright	
Seven Initial Carvers of Boston 1700-1725	210
Theodore Chase and Laurel K. Gabel	
Contributors	233
Index	235

Figure 1. Elizabeth Sinclair, 1785, New Haven.
Unless otherwise noted, all stones are attributed to Thomas Gold, and are in Connecticut.

"MD. BY THOS. GOLD":
THE GRAVESTONES OF A NEW HAVEN CARVER

Meredith M. Williams and Gray Williams, Jr.

In the middle of New Haven, Connecticut, across Grove Street from the campus of Yale University, lies the New Haven Burying Ground, better known as the Grove Street Cemetery. It was founded in 1796, and most of its graves are of the 19th and 20th centuries. But it also contains a substantial number of earlier gravestones, some erected in the cemetery itself, some propped up against the northern and western walls. These were moved from an earlier burying ground on New Haven Green, a couple of blocks away, and make up one of the largest collections of 18th-century stones in Connecticut.

Many of these stones, dating from the 1770s to 1800, share a distinctive, easily recognizable style (figure 1). The carving is simple, linear, and highly stylized, yet skillful and refined. The head of the soul effigy is a smooth, symmetrical oval -- nearly round in earlier examples, narrower and more egg-shaped in later ones. Within this frame, the features are relatively small, the close-set eyes and narrow, unsmiling mouth conveying a rather worried-looking expression. The feathers of the flanking wings are rendered as curving parallel bands, decorated with a pattern of repeated S- or C-shaped incisions. Between the shoulders of the wings, and sometimes touching them, is fitted the "Crown of Righteousness" typical of Connecticut carving. The inscription is usually bordered on each side by a panel containing a foliage design: a fern fiddlehead at the top, surmounting stylized buds and leaves. The same design continues across the base, in the middle of which is a small, neat heart (figure 2).

To find the name of this carver is not difficult. In the former chapel of the cemetery, now its office, is preserved his single signed stone (figure 3). A fairly elaborate example of his work, it is the memorial of Caleb Hotchkiss, killed in a punitive raid by the British in 1779. Below the main inscription appears "Md. by Thos. Gold."

Figure 2. Detail of Elizabeth Sinclair stone, showing heart design in bottom border.

Figure 3. Caleb Hotchkiss, 1779, New Haven. Signed by Thomas Gold. Rubbing by Anne Williams and Susan Kelly.

Thomas Gold was a popular and prolific carver. There are almost 170 of his stones at the Grove Street Cemetery alone, and his work is strongly represented in the graveyards of New Haven and Fairfield counties, with substantial groups as far off as Woodbury in Litchfield County to the north, and Long Island, New York, to the south. We have counted well over 600 stones that can be safely attributed to him, and our list is not complete (see Table 1). Moreover, the fragmentary nature of several of these stones suggests that there may once have been many more than now survive. Without question, Gold was the leading sculptor of this particular area in the last part of the 18th century.

Surprisingly little has been written or published about Gold. In 1974 Morris Abbott outlined the main elements of his style, in a pamphlet based on the stones in the Milford Cemetery.[1] In 1976, David Corrigan published a biographical sketch,[2] and later provided further information to Richard Welch, included in the latter's study of Long Island gravestones.[3] Perhaps most important of all, the indefatigable Ernest Caulfield made extensive observations of Gold's work, and did invaluable research on Gold's probated stones; his notes were unpublished at his death, but fortunately have been preserved by James Slater.[4]

But none of these researchers attempted an evaluation of Gold's entire career, or of the variations in his style (such as his excursion into neoclassicism, in his last years). None attempted to identify the influence of the carver Michael Baldwin on Gold's early career, or the significant influence of Gold, in turn, upon the neoclassic carver David Ritter. And none attempted to separate Gold's own work from that of possible associates and imitators. This essay is intended to fill in some of the gaps, and to demonstrate Gold's place in the history of Connecticut carving.

The Documentary Record

Thomas Gold was not a prominent person in 18th-century Connecticut. Only a few documents, such as census reports, church birth and death records, and land and estate records, provide us with sketchy details of his life and career. He was born in the coastal town of Stratford in 1733.[5] He came from a family of ministers: his father, Hezekiah, was a Congregational minister in Stratford, and his mother, Mary Ruggles, was the daughter of the Reverend Thomas Ruggles of Guilford. His only brother, Hezekiah, two years his senior, led a congregation in Cornwall. Thomas, however, did not train for the ministry, and consequently did not attend Harvard (as his father had) or follow his brother to Yale.[6] In 1755, he married Anna (or Anne) Smith of Redding, and lived there at least until the death of his father in 1761; the latter's will mentions a "son Thomas at Redding."[7] Some time after, he moved to nearby Danbury; from there, in 1772, he moved to New Haven.[8]

Gold arrived in the company of a congregation of Sandemanians -- that is, followers of Scottish theologian Robert Sandeman.[9] At the time of his death, the inventory of Gold's possessions listed "2 vol. Theron," referring to *Letters on Theron and Aspasio*, Sandeman's most influential treatise, published in 1757.[10] Essentially fundamentalists, the Sandemanians rejected the concept of a salaried ministry. Instead, they established independent congregations led by groups of "elders," basing their services upon the literal reconstruction of devotional practices described in the Bible. They also insisted that their members give to charity all but the most essential portion of their income.[11]

The Sandemanians discouraged communication with other denominations. The rift between their church and the orthodox Christian community is evident in a *Connecticut Journal* advertisement of March 5, 1773, which announced "Proposals for Reprinting by Subscription, a Discourse on Justification by Faith Alone by Reverend Jonathan Edwards, esteemed by the best judges to be an excellent antidote to many erroneous doctrines prevalent in the country, both Arminian and Sandemanian." [12] Moreover, Sandemanian adherence to scriptural commandments regarding obedience to rulers would translate, during the Revolution, into continued loyalty to the Crown, causing further conflict between the sect and its Connecticut neighbors.[13]

Gold probably belonged to one of the "Dozen Sandemanian Families" reported by Ezra Stiles to have settled in New Haven in the spring of 1772, under the leadership of elders Titus Smith and Theophilus Chamberlain, both Yale-educated ministers.[14] Gold was closely affiliated with Chamberlain, with whom he purchased a small lot in 1774, presumably a storefront, as it was only 30 feet wide and faced the Town Street.[15] In a lawsuit brought against Sam Spelman of Wallingford, the two men referred to themselves as "Gold and Chamberlain, Merchants in Company," and a biography of Chamberlain confirms that he "kept a country store for a short time (in company with Thomas Gold in 1774)."[16]

But about the same time, Gold was also carving gravestones. The 1775 probate record for the estate of Abner Judson (who died in 1774) includes the following: "Paid to Thomas Gold for gravestones," and the amount: 3 pounds, 18 shillings.[17]

It is quite likely that, like other carvers, Gold supported himself with more than one occupation. For instance, fellow stonecutter Michael Baldwin, who was established in New Haven from about 1769, was at the same time a blacksmith, rate collector, tavern keeper, real estate investor, and landlord. Baldwin did very well from his combined occupations. In addition to large land holdings, he left an estate worth 1510 pounds at his death in 1787.[18]

In 1777, the Sandemanians rejected a demand by the Connecticut legislature that they pledge to refuse aid to the British military effort. There is no evidence that the Sandemanians had actually collaborated with the British, but they wouldn't promise not to. As a result, many were forced to leave New Haven for British-occupied New York.[19] Gold may have been one of the group of Sandemanians who were reported by Ezra Stiles to be "embarking for Long Island" in November.[20]

That Gold did indeed leave Connecticut during the war is at least suggested by the probate record for John Brooks of Stratford, who died in March 1777 (See Appendix A). The stone Gold carved for him (figure 6) can safely be assigned to this period, as will be shown later. But Gold did not get paid for his work until 1788; perhaps the long delay was in part the result of extended absence from the area.

Gold appears to have returned to Connecticut even before the war formally ended. Probate records indicate that he was paid to carve a stone for Edward Hawley of Stratford in 1782. He received payment for the stone of Samuel Willcockson, or Wilcoxson, the following year, and the probate records document eleven more payments from customers in the New Haven area, right up until the year of Gold's own death in 1800. Incidentally, the spellings in these records suggest strongly that his name may have been pronounced "Gould" (see Appendix A).

After the war, Gold appears to have settled again in New Haven. Land records of 1789 show a transaction between Gold and Mary MacLean of Windsor, for "a certain brick house in the city of New Haven," located on Fleet Street, which extended from the corner of what are now State and George Streets.[21] This house can be traced back in land records through Mary MacLean's family; it can also be found on the 1748 plan of New Haven, under the name of one of her ancestors, John Prout. The following year, 1790, Gold relinquished one sixth of his claim to "Mary (Sloan) Mac-Clean,"[22] but he continued to occupy the house. Described as Gold's dwelling in the inventory of his possessions at his death,[23] it was probably his workshop as well, for it contained "Grave Stones, [valued at] 40 [pounds];" as well as "2 Hammers, Gimblets and Brush," valued at 2 shillings altogether; "one Stone," possibly a grindstone, "3 [shillings];" and "Engraving Tools, 9 [shillings]."

In 1796, Gold also purchased, for 30 pounds, five acres on "ye Oyster Point;"[24] he may have been attempting to supplement his income by engaging in the oyster trade that developed after the war.[25] In any event, he sold the land two years later, at a profit of five pounds.[26]

Gold died March 22, 1800, at the age of 67.[27] His estate was valued at 221 pounds, 12 shillings -- a relatively small amount, compared with the estate of Michael Baldwin 13 years earlier. Gold was evidently not as active a businessman, and perhaps he had taken to heart the Sandemanian admonition not to "lay up treasures on earth." He was survived only briefly by his wife, who died two months later.[28] There is no record of any children, although the 1790 census lists a second white female (possibly a servant) in the household.[29]

Figure 4. Abner Judson, 1774, Stratford. Probated stone.

Early Works -- The Baldwin Influence

The stone for Abner Judson (figure 4), for which Gold was paid in 1775, is the earliest existing stone for which a probate record is available. It is the work of an already accomplished, fully professional carver, and how Gold came to such command of his craft is something of a mystery. The only stones that might be described as novice works form a group of about half a dozen small examples located in Danbury (where Gold lived up to 1772) and in nearby Bethel. They are all made of a coarse, pinkish-gray local stone, which was probably cheap, and would have made good practice material. It was not very durable, though, and weathering has made most of these stones almost totally illegible.

The best-preserved of this group, the stone for Eliakim Davis in Bethel (figure 5), closely resembles the Abner Judson stone in design. It is much smaller, though, and its surface, even before weathering, must have been very rough. It is dated 1776, and none of the others in the group carries a date earlier than 1774. If these do indeed represent early works, carved before Gold moved to New Haven, then he must have lettered them years later -- possibly when he got customers for them from among his former neighbors.

The Abner Judson stone has Gold's typical foliage border, described earlier. The soul effigy, however, differs from Gold's usual style. Similar effigies appear on several other stones of the 1770s, such as the probated stone for John Brooks, who died in 1777 (figure 6); the stone for Gold's sister Hulda Curtis and her infant daughter, who died in 1765 (figure 7); and the multi-effigy stone for the six children of his sister Mary Tomlinson, bearing the date 1771 (figure 8). The faces, and even more so the wings, of these effigies strongly resemble the work of Michael Baldwin (figures 9-11). Baldwin was 15 years Gold's senior, and had been an established stonecutter in New Haven since 1769. It would have been quite natural for Gold to have modeled his early work on Baldwin's, as much to maximize his chances of selling his own work as to master the gravestone craft.

Figure 5. Eliakim Davis, 1776, Bethel.

Figure 6. John Brooks, 1777, Stratford. Probated stone.

Figure 7. Hulda Curtis and infant daughter, 1765, Stratford.

Figure 8. Mary Alice Tomlinson, 1771, and five other Tomlinson children, Stratford.

There is one other stylistic element that Gold might have derived from Baldwin: the use of linear drawing and simple, flat planes, in place of three-dimensional modeling. Not necessarily, though: this simplified, rather diminished style is typical of late 18th-century carving in general, and there are plenty of other examples that Gold might have seen. It may have been the result of economic pressures rather than lack of skill or talent -- the linear style would have been quicker to execute, and therefore more economical. In at least one instance, as we shall see, Gold demonstrated that he was quite capable of carving in subtle relief when he wished to do so.

The association between Gold and Michael Baldwin may have been closer than mere influence and imitation. Baldwin's dwelling house was on the Town Street, as was Gold's store.[30] Gold carved a stone for one of Baldwin's sons, who died in 1776. And when Baldwin himself died, in 1787, Gold carved his stone as well (figure 38).

Figure 9. Ebenezer Silliman, 1775, Fairfield.
Probated stone by Michael Baldwin.

Figure 10. John Miller, 1770, New Haven.
Attributed to Michael Baldwin.

**Figure 11. Job Prudden, 1774, Milford.
Attributed to Michael Baldwin.**

But from the beginning, there were distinctive differences in Gold's style, even when he was imitating Baldwin. Although the general configuration of the faces might be similar, Gold made his features smaller in proportion to the head, and almost never put pupils in the eyes. Furthermore, Baldwin often extended the central septum of the nose downward in a distinctive loop, almost suggesting a ring between the nostrils (figure 11), a device never used by Gold. And although Gold sometimes adopted foliage borders rather like Baldwin's (figures 5-8), they are generally simpler, and less incisively carved.

The lettering styles of the two carvers, though basically similar, also differ in recognizable ways. In general, Baldwin's lettering style (figure 10) is broader, more spontaneous, and less uniform than Gold's. Baldwin's characters tend to be more deeply carved, with more pronounced serifs, so that the bases of his letters, especially his f's, form triangles. Baldwin's numeral 8's are twice the x-height, while Gold's stay within this limit. Unlike Baldwin, Gold often carved his 5's and 3's with exaggerated diagonal slashes. Gold often inserted a joined and italicized "AD" before the date of death, a device seldom used by Baldwin. And whereas Gold's italic f's are nearly vertical, Baldwin's slant dramatically forward.

Even more important is a difference in the basic layout of the inscriptions, which results in differences in certain key letters. Both men lightly scribed parallel rows of horizontal guidelines before starting to chisel the characters. Weathering has often obliterated these lines, but they remain quite evident, for example, on Baldwin's slate stone for Job Prudden (figure 11). Baldwin's guidelines are evenly spaced, so the ascenders and descenders are the same size as the x-height. Gold, apparently to separate the lines of characters more distinctly, drew his guidelines with shortened spaces for the ascenders and descenders. Consequently, Gold's g's and y's tend to be noticeably shallower and stubbier than Baldwin's.

**Figure 12. Rebeckah Tomlinson, 1774, Stratford.
Attributed to Michael Baldwin.**

Despite these differences, there are a few works, such as the stone for Rebeckah Tomlinson (figure 12), where it is difficult, if not impossible, to make a firm attribution to either carver alone. Did Gold and Baldwin work together, either as partners, or as apprentice and master? Without documentation, one cannot say for sure.

Early Works -- Other Influences

Side by side in the Grove Street Cemetery in New Haven are the gravestones of John and Mary Howell, who died within three months of each other in 1776 (figures 13 and 14). Since the stones are about the same size, one may presume that they were carved together, as a pair. Both also display the typical Gold border, and Gold's characteristic lettering style.

The stone for John Howell is so similar, in every respect, to the probated Abner Judson stone (figure 4) that it could be attributed to Gold on that basis. The soul effigy on the stone for Mary Howell (figure 14), however, is rather different. The head is larger and more oblong, and is surmounted by a band of stylized hair. The wings do not at all resemble Baldwin's, but are composed of parallel bands symbolizing rows of feathers, with individual feathers suggested by repeated S-curves. In this particular example the wings join under the chin, and are connected by a round, buttonlike knot. Since all the other details correspond so exactly with those on the companion stone, it seems safe to attribute this one to Gold as well. But it is evident that he was following other models besides Baldwin in these early years.

Earlier stones in the New Haven area suggest what these models might have been. The stone for Elisabeth Willford in Branford (figure 15) is typical of a number of works by an unknown Connecticut carver active in the 1750s and 1760s. The banded wings of the soul effigy, with their S-shaped feather marks, and the crown that fits neatly between them, are very similar to those carved by Gold. Even more important, this carver seems to have provided the model for Gold's distinctive foliage border. Gold's own rendering of all these motifs, though, is at once more abstract, more refined, and more skillful -- qualities that are hallmarks of his style.

Figure 13. John Howell, 1776, New Haven.

Figure 14. Mary Howell, 1776, New Haven.

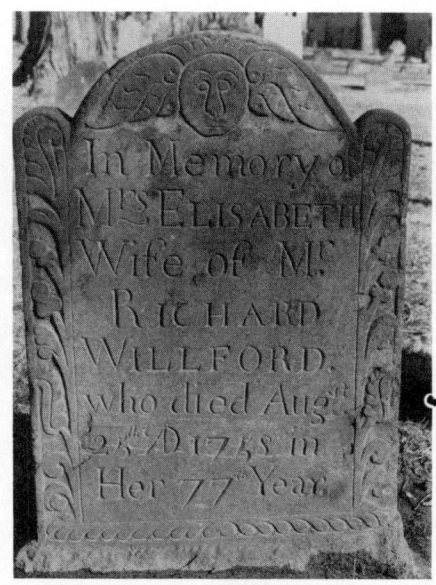

Figure 15. Elisabeth Willford, 1758, Branford. Carver unknown.

Another unknown artist, who carved the Roswell and Huldah Woodward stones in East Haven (figure 16), may have given Gold the idea for the wings joined under the chin -- or both he and Gold might have been drawing from some other source. In any event, it is plain that Gold, like virtually every other carver of his time, developed his own style by imitating and improvising upon the work of others, and that, in the early part of his career, he experimented with a variety of motifs.

On the basis of the Mary Howell stone (figure 14), a number of others dated in the 1770s can be attributed to Gold. Some resemble the Howell stone in every detail, such as the stone for Gold's brother-in-law Agur Tomlinson (figure 17). In some, such as the stone for David Perkins (figure 18), the banded wings appear to sprout from the sides of the head. A few display unusual variations, such as the elaborate, turbanlike crown that appears on the stone for Benjamin Douglas (figure 19). And although most share Gold's typical border, some -- particularly some small stones for children -- contain a quite different design: a simple, curvilinear vine-and-leaf pattern (figure 20). This design, as we shall see later, becomes important in attributing still another body of work.

Figure 16. Huldah Woodward, 1773, East Haven. Carver unknown.

Figure 17. Agur Tomlinson, 1774, Stratford.

Figure 18. David Perkins, 1776, Woodbridge.

Figure 19. Benjamin Douglas, 1775, New Haven. Detail of tympanum.

Figure 20. Elias Parmele, 1773, New Haven.

One stone in this style is of particular interest in light of Gold's connection with the loyalist Sandemanians. Among several memorials that Gold carved for the Sanford family in Redding is one for Daniel Sanford and his son Jeremiah, both of whom died in the summer of 1777 (figure 21). Jeremiah, the inscription reads, "died a Prisoner in New York." It seems most unlikely that Gold would have been given this commission if he had been known as a strong supporter of the British. The stone suggests that Gold's loyalty to the Crown may have been lukewarm at best, and that he may have retained his personal ties to his American neighbors.

It would also explain why he was able to return to Connecticut as the war was ending -- many other New Haven Sandemanians emigrated either to Canada or other parts of New England.[31] It might also explain why he was able to become an even more popular carver there than before. As noted earlier, there is probate-record evidence of his presence as early as 1782, when he executed the stone for Edward Hawley in Stratford (figure 22), and in 1783, when he was paid for the stone of Samuel Willcockson (figure 23).

Figure 21. Daniel and Jeremiah Sanford, 1777, Redding.

The stone he carved and signed for war victim Caleb Hotchkiss (figure 3), is very much like Willcockson's, and appears to have been done about the same time. Perhaps Gold made a point of signing that particular stone to demonstrate his political neutrality, and to advertise to potential customers that he was "back in business."

These stones of the 1780s display slight but distinct changes in Gold's style. The lettering remains much the same, except for a wider lower-case y. The distinctive foliage border is indistinguishable from those carved earlier. The most noticeable change is in the proportions of the soul effigy: the head becomes narrower, and so do the features within it. The head and wings are often set off from the rest of the stone by a deeply chiseled trench. The crown is more widely flared, and there is the suggestion of a small heart shape in the center, seeming to echo that in the bottom border. The feather marks on the wings are shaped like C rather than S. And in the postwar works, the wings, without exception, start at the sides of the head, and no longer appear joined beneath the chin. This last is an especially important change, as will now be shown.

Figure 22. Edward Hawley, 1782, Stratford. Probated stone.

Figure 23. Samuel Willcockson, 1783, Stratford. Probated stone.

**Figure 24. Ruth Beard, 1778, Derby.
Attributed to the Derby Carver.**

The "Derby Carver"

There are at least 60 stones that can be safely identified as Gold's work up through 1777 (see Table 1, p. 54). More than 70 others bear dates as early as these, but are plainly in Gold's postwar style, and presumably backdated. In addition, there is still another group of some 48 stones, bearing dates from 1773 to 1788, which in the past have usually been attributed to Gold.[32] For several reasons we question this attribution, and believe that the stones should be assigned to another carver.

The most striking characteristic of the group as a whole (figures 24-30) is the face shape of the soul effigy. The head is quite round, with a narrow, almost pointed chin. The eyes, particularly in the later examples, are much larger, and the nose broader, than the same features in Gold's work. Although the overall effect does not look radically different from the various soul-effigy forms carved by Gold himself, it is nonetheless distinctive.

Another different motif is a border that appears on several of these stones (figure 24). Superficially, it looks like the curved vine designs that Gold occasionally used (figures 20, 31, 32), but comparison shows that it is far more angular, spiky, and crude in execution.

In one other aspect of design, these stones depart at least partly from Gold's work. On every stone in this group, from early to late, and without exception, the wings meet under the chin in a buttonlike knot. The same design can be found on a number of Gold's *prewar* stones (figures 14, 17, 21), but we have never found it on any of his stones dated after 1777.

There are also some slight but recognizable differences in lettering style. The bells of letters such as lower-case p and b, and capital D, are widened and flattened at the bottom -- giving them a rather bottom-heavy look. Capital A tends to be somewhat wider, and has a higher crossbar than is usual on Gold's stones. Capital H is definitely wider, and its crossbar never displays the "star" motif that Gold often uses. Particularly distinctive is lower-case italic *h*: it is so rounded at the bottom that it could easily be taken for *b*.

In general, the lettering in this group of stones seems to be somewhat sloppier and more prone to error than the lettering on stones that can be attributed to Gold. Not that Gold did not make mistakes. On the stone for his sister Hulda, for instance (figure 7), he left out the r in "memory," and made no effort to correct it. Likewise, on the stone for Daniel and Jeremiah Sanford (figure 21), "his" is misspelled "whis," again with no effort at cover-up or correction. Nonetheless, the lettering in this special group seems to have an even higher proportion of errors, combined with a tendency to correct them with clumsy overwriting, as, for example, on the stone for Elizabeth Royce (figure 25).

Finally, although probated stones form only a small percentage of the hundreds of works that can be ascribed to Gold, it is perhaps significant that not one of them is in the style of this special group. In any event, all the evidence adds up to suggest that these stones are by another hand.

But we do not know whose hand it might be, and we must acknowledge that this other artist must have been closely associated with Gold, at least in the 1770s. The stylistic differences in such elements as lettering are subtle rather than obvious, and there are several early works by the unknown carver that include such Gold "trademarks" as his foliage border, topped with fern fiddleheads (figure 25).

Moreover, at least one stone, the stone for Mindwell Rice (figure 26) appears to have a design carved by Gold, but lettering in the style of the unknown carver. Conversely, the elaborate stone for Anne Williams (figure 27) has the soul effigy typical of the unknown carver, but it also has the typical Gold border, and its long inscription seems to have been lettered by Gold. Our belief is that the unknown carver worked with Gold at least occasionally before the war, but then struck out completely on his own.

This hypothesis is given some support by evidence from geography and dating (see Table 1). Stones of the 1770s by the unknown carver appear in a number of graveyards in and around New Haven. In some places, such as New Haven itself, East Haven, and Wallingford, the unknown carver and Gold are both well represented. But other graveyards which contain a number of early Gold stones have few or none by the unknown carver; these include Stratford, Woodbridge, Danbury, and Redding. And still others contain several works of the unknown carver, but few or no early works by Gold himself; these include North Haven, Northford, Fairfield, and Derby.

Figure 25. Elizabeth Royce, 1775, Wallingford. Attributed to the Derby Carver. Photograph by Daniel and Jessie Lie Farber.

Figure 26. Mindwell Rice, 1776, Meriden. Decoration attributed to Thomas Gold. Lettering attributed to the Derby Carver. Photograph by Daniel and Jessie Lie Farber.

Figure 27. Anne Williams, 1776, Northford. Decoration attributed to the Derby Carver. Lettering attributed to Thomas Gold.

Figure 28. Joseph Hull, 1775, Derby. Attributed to the Derby Carver.

Derby stands out in particular. The Old Burying Ground there contains half a dozen stones by this carver, and no early stones by Gold at all. One stone, moreover, the elaborate memorial for Joseph Hull (figure 28), is among the finest examples of the unknown artist's work. We therefore call him, for convenience, the Derby Carver.

After the war, when Gold's work turns up in a much wider range of Connecticut communities, stones by the Derby Carver appear almost entirely in New Haven, plus single examples in East Haven and Milford (figure 30). There are none at all dated after 1788, whereas Gold kept on carving right up to 1800. Moreover, the Derby Carver's stones of the 1780s are much more uneven in quality than those carved before the war, whereas Gold's own work became even more expert and refined.

Figure 29. Wilhelmus Stoothoff, 1783, Brooklyn, New York. Attributed to the Derby Carver. Photograph by Richard Welch.

There is also some rather special evidence from New York. In the general vicinity of New York City, there is a small group of stones by the Derby Carver, bearing dates from 1778 to 1783 (figure 29). In contrast, there are no corresponding stones that can be attributed to Gold himself (see Table 1). It appears that although Gold may have gone to New York during the war, he may not have done any carving there; whereas his associate -- whether or not he was a Sandemanian -- not only relocated in New York, but continued to carve there at least until 1783.

**Figure 30. Susannah Miles, 1788, Milford.
Attributed to the Derby Carver.**

This is a subject that needs further research -- especially in areas such as New York and western Connecticut where the Derby Carver may have worked on his own, and where he seems to have had a number of imitators. Further documentary research might still produce his name, or else incontrovertible proof that we are mistaken, and that Gold himself was the carver of these stones. From the evidence available to us, however, we judge that virtually all of them are the work of an early associate of Gold, who worked with him before the war, went to New York during the war to continue carving independently, and returned to New Haven afterward, ending his career in the late 1780s.

Postwar Works

As mentioned earlier, probate records place Gold back in Connecticut in 1782. We do not know whether he went straight back to New Haven; there is no record of his having bought property there until 1789. The probated stones of 1782 and 1783 are both for citizens of Gold's home town of Stratford; perhaps he settled there for awhile.

But without question, he became even more active as a carver than he had been before the war. There are 60 stones of the 1770s that can be attributed to him; from the postwar years, between 1782 and 1800, the number approaches 600 (see Table 1).

It is evident that Gold's reputation spread more widely as well. His work of the 1770s is largely concentrated in those communities where he lived and had personal contacts: New Haven, where he first established himself as a professional carver; his home town of Stratford; the village of Redding, where he lived for several years following his marriage; and Danbury, where he lived before moving to New Haven. But substantial numbers of his postwar stones appear in many other communities of New Haven and Fairfield Counties, including Branford, East Haven, West Haven, North Haven, Northford, Woodbridge, Bethany, Milford, Shelton, and Newtown. They also turn up over a much wider area, including several across Long Island Sound in Suffolk County, New York.

The main elements of Gold's postwar style have already been summarized. In general, his work of the 1780s and 1790s shows greater professional polish and standardization. He no longer carved imitations of Michael Baldwin, except for occasional footstones (figure 31). He did design a new and even more graceful curved-vine border design, with tendrils ending in three leaves or berries; he used it mainly on relatively small works such as footstones and the memorials for children (figure 32). On stones of the later 1780s and after, he sometimes used much simplified borders (figure 33), or none at all.

One unusual and rather curious design that appears on a few of Gold's postwar stones is a pair of joined heads (figure 32), used exclusively for the double memorials of children. What the source and meaning (if any) of this device were we do not know; it seems to convey a rather touching sense of spiritual kinship. Perhaps, though, Gold used it simply to cut down on the amount of carving needed for two complete images.

Figure 31. Footstone for Alice Wyatt, Fairfield.

Figure 32. Mary Gilbert, 1758, and Rebecca Gilbert, 1776, New Haven.

Figure 33. Lydia Thompson, 1786, New Haven.

The lettering on the postwar stones is somewhat more even and uniform, but continues to be unusually afflicted with typographical errors. The problem arose out of Gold's customary working procedure: he appears not to have laid out his inscriptions in advance. Instead, he "wrote with the chisel," usually starting at a fixed left margin, and adjusting the spacing between letters and words as he went along. It is a tribute to his craftsmanship that the results turned out as well as they did.

Sometimes Gold made a kind of first draft, engraving the inscription lightly, and then going back over it, to correct any mistakes the second time around (figure 34). Sometimes, if the lettering was carved lightly, he could "erase" a mistake by grinding down the area in which it occurred and then carving over it. But he could almost never conceal the insertion of a missing letter (figure 35), and sometimes his corrections are embarrassingly crude (figure 36).

Figure 34. Thomas Beecher, 1787, Woodbridge. Detail of inscription.

Figure 35. Mabel Bradley, 1798, Woodbridge.

Figure 36. Ebenezer Sherman, 1764, Stratford.

Economics played a part: the bigger and more expensive stones generally contain fewer errors. On some of these, all or part of the inscription is centered, which probably required more advance preparation, and provided more opportunity to catch mistakes before they were, quite literally, engraved in stone. But there are exceptions even here. For example, Gold was commissioned to carve a fairly imposing set of headstones and footstones for Ebenezer and Esther Hickok of Bethel. It is plausible that Gold received his intructions in writing, and misread the family name as "Hiekok." He rendered it thus, in unambiguous capitals, and then had to amend it, on all four stones (figure 37).

As before the war, Gold carved quite a range of stones, in terms of both size and complexity of design. The simplest were footstones, and modest stones for small children. At the other end of the scale were tablets that were larger and more elaborate than just about any he carved earlier. One of these is the monument for the carver who originally inspired him, Michael Baldwin (figure 38). As on other large stones, the usual crown is replaced by a stylized keystone, so that the tympanum recalls the broken-pediment form often used in rococo architecture; this is in fact a device that Gold borrowed from Baldwin (figure 9).

Particularly in Gold's postwar work, certain verses turn up over and over. Some of these were part of the standard repertoire, such as the verse often appearing on monuments for children:

> Sleep, lovely babe, and take thy rest.
> God called thee home because He thought it best.

But in some instances, the choice may reflect Gold's personal taste, such as the following quotation from Revelations (XIV, 13), which appears, either complete or abridged, on many of Gold's stones:

> Blessed are the dead who die in the Lord. Even so, saith the Spirit, for they rest in their labors and their works shall follow them.

Figure 37. Ebenezer Hickock, 1774, Bethel.

Figure 38. Michael Baldwin, 1787, New Haven.

And there is at least one verse for which we have been unable to find either a literary source (other than a general reference to Revelations), or any other appearance in gravestone carving:

> The Woman's Seed Shall Bruise the Serpent's Head,
> And Christ Shall raise his Servants from the Dead.

Such examples suggest that Gold may have supplied his customers with choices in verses as well as in decorations.

In the 1790s, Gold made further slight alterations to his standard soul effigy. The heads become even narrower, the chins more pointed, and they are often set off from the background by a double outline. Sometimes small, stylized ears are added. On the wings, there are more crescent-shaped marks to suggest feathers. Below, the lettering tends to be laid out with more attention to spacing and centering. The probated stone for Mary Merwin (figure 39), is a good example of these characteristics.

Figure 39. Mary Merwin, 1797, Milford. Probated stone.

Mary Merwin's headstone and footstone are significant in one other respect: they are executed in slate. This was a very unusual material for Connectictut carvers, and Gold appears to have come upon it only late in his career.

From the 1770s and into the 1780s, Gold, like most other carvers of central Connecticut, worked almost exclusively in sandstone. We do not know exactly what his sources were, but there were sandstone quarries in the New Haven area, plus a number of well-known ones in the Connecticut River valley. In the 1780s, Gold used not only several varieties of the common red sandstone, but an unusual yellow form as well (figure 32), relatively durable, but with an unhappy tendency to discolor.

Then, starting as early as a probated stone for Benajah Peck in Bethany, paid for in 1787, Gold began working in marble as well. At the time marble, with its associations with classical antiquity, doubtless seemed both more elegant and more permanent than sandstone. Several of Gold's monuments bear inscriptions like this: "Engraved in Marble is the Memory of Agur Judson, Esqr." (figure 40). Unfortunately for Mr. Judson and for Gold, marble suffers from our acid climate, and decomposes far more rapidly than sandstone. Almost all of Gold's marbles are rough, granulated, and nearly illegible.

Could Gold have known this would happen? Almost certainly not. Yet the ruin of his marble stones was hastened and aggravated by the particular kind of stone he used. Furthermore, the nature of the stone was evident at the time Gold cut it.

We know this from a uniquely preserved group of stones located in the crypt of the Center Church on New Haven Green. As indicated earlier, the Green was used as the city burying ground until the end of the 18th century. Many of the stones were then moved to the new Grove Street Cemetery -- but not all at once. In 1813, when famed New Haven architect Ithiel Town built Center Church in the middle of the Green, that part of the old burying ground was apparently still intact. So the foundation walls of the church were simply built around it, and the first floor raised high enough to form a crypt beneath. And there the stones of the old burying ground have remained, in their original positions, ever since.

Figure 40. Agur Judson, 1791, Shelton.

Among the more than 150 stones, there are 29 that can be attributed to Gold (including two probated examples -- see Appendix A). Eight of these are of marble, and since none can have been much over 25 years in the open air, they look as if they had just been carved. And they are beautifully crafted. The surfaces are milled to a satiny smoothness; the chisel work is crisp and even. No wonder Gold was attracted to this material, and was able (or so the probate records suggest) to charge a premium price for it.

But if you look closely, you can see that the marble Gold used is not homogeneous. Rather, it is composed of granules in a matrix of less durable material. It is this matrix which has eroded worst in the outdoor stones, ravaging the carving, and leaving the surface rough, grainy, and so downright ugly that one could hardly imagine why the material was ever appealing -- were it not for the pristine stones in the crypt.

Some time in the 1790s, Gold added slate to the materials in which he worked. We do not know where he obtained it; neither slate nor marble were quarried nearby. Michael Baldwin used slate for at least one stone, possibly backdated 1774 (figure 11). The slate used by Gold is fine-grained and well preserved, and ranges in color from a light gray-blue to an even lighter, creamy gray with a slightly greenish tinge. Slate suited Gold's meticulous style, and in it he executed some of his finest works.

An unusual and revealing example is the stone for Eunice Cook, dated 1794 (figure 41). Virtually all of Gold's soul effigies are basically linear and two dimensional, with little effort at modeling. This is a remarkable exception. The wings and crown are typical, but the face is much more realistic than usual, and skillfully modeled in low relief. On the shoulders, also in low relief, are delicately carved oak leaves. The design is clearly an imitation of the sophisticated slate monuments carved in the Boston area, and may have been modeled upon the stone for Gold's father, which bears a similar face (figure 42). Presumably the stone was a special commission, made for a customer who wanted a stone of the Boston type, but who for some reason did not choose to import it. In any event, it demonstrates that Gold was familiar with cosmopolitan styles, and was quite capable of executing more sophisticated work if he chose to do so.

Figure 41. Eunice Cook, 1794, Woodbridge.

Figure 42. Hezekiah Gold, 1761, Stratford.
Attributed to Boston area carver.

Figure 43. Martha Pond, 1797, Milford.

Figure 44. Martha Miles, 1797, Milford.

Neoclassic Stones

From the beginning of his career, Gold had carved crowned soul effigies of the typical Connecticut form. But starting with a stone dated 1793, he began to carve a neoclassic design as well: a cinerary urn in three-dimensional relief, surmounted by a ropelike swag and two stylized flowers (figures 43, 45, 46). There is no evidence of experiment or transition -- no cautious attempt to incorporate the new motif into his traditional designs. He did not even use his trademark foliage border on these stones, but only a simple band or a beaded edge. The stones are completely of the new style, with its patriotic associations between the young American republic and its noble antecedents in ancient Greece and Rome.

Gold did not make a complete switch to the new style: he continued to carve soul effigies, and he carved both designs in sandstone, marble, and slate (see Table 2). For example, there is a group of five stones at Milford whose general proximity to one another, and whose similar inscriptions (all begin with the curious wording, "Entomb'd is here deposited the Dear remains of...") suggest that they all formed part of a single family commission. They include both urn and soul-effigy designs in slate, and a soul effigy in sandstone (figures 43, 44).

Figure 45. James Gilbert, 1798, New Haven. Probated stone.

Figure 46. Tympanum of James Gilbert stone.

The only probated example of Gold's urn design may well have been his last commission (figures 45, 46). On February 27, 1800, he was paid four pounds ten shillings for the memorial of Deacon James Gilbert, and he himself died a month later, on March 22. The stone is an especially fine example of his work, crisply and elegantly carved in slate pale enough to suggest marble. The lettering, both in layout and execution, is notably harmonious and graceful. If this is indeed Gold's last work, it demonstrates that his skill and talent remained undiminished right up to the end of his life.

After Gold's death, his brother-in-law Levi Hubbard was appointed to administer his estate. He was succeeded by two of Gold's nephews, who attended to its final settlement. Apparently Gold had no children, and his wife died two months after he did.[33] The items of greatest value in the inventory of his property were his house, valued at 90 pounds, and 40 pounds' worth of gravestones.[34] The house was sold to David Ritter, who belonged to the third generation of a family of Connecticut stonecutters.[35] Ritter also appears to have acquired Gold's unfinished gravestones. What happened to them forms a fascinating postscript to the story of Gold's career.

The Ritter Connection

Despite the large number of stones that can be attributed to Thomas Gold, there is little evidence of the aid of any associate or apprentice. There are two exceptions. One is the anonymous Derby Carver, discussed earlier, who was apparently associated with Gold toward the beginning of his career. The other is a carver whose name we do know, and who became significant at the end of Gold's career.

In the Grove Street Cemetery in New Haven, the stone for Lydie Atwater (figure 47), has a tympanum and border that are plainly carved by Gold. But the lettering, with its shorter proportions and wider serifs, is by another hand entirely. The same carver attempted some soul effigies of his own (figure 48), at once more realistic and more clumsy than Gold's elegant abstractions.

This carver later became much more skillful, in the neoclassic style. But his lettering remained essentially the same. From his signed works (figure 49) we can identify him as David Ritter, the man who bought Gold's house.

Figure 47. Lydie Atwater, 1784, New Haven. Decoration attributed to Thomas Gold. Lettering attributed to David Ritter.

Figure 48. Jonathan Cutler, 1776, New Haven. Attributed to David Ritter.

Figure 49. Chloe Meigs, 1788, Madison. Signed by David Ritter.

Starting in the 1790s, David Ritter, like Gold, began carving urn designs, often surmounted by swags and flowers (figure 50). But there are noticeable differences in detail between Ritter's and Gold's renderings of the same basic design. These differences are significant, as will be shown.

At Grove street is a rather mysterious stone for two children of the Ives family (figure 51). The tympanum is decorated with a pair of typical Gold soul effigies, but the inscription bears a date in 1801, about a year and a half after Gold's death. The lettering provides the solution to the puzzle: it is by Ritter, and the stone is evidently one of those he bought, already decorated but not yet lettered, from Gold's estate.

It was, of course, customary for carvers to prepare an inventory of decorated stones, which could later be lettered for specific customers. That Gold followed this practice is suggested by a decorated but uninscribed stone in East Haven (figure 52): it is the size of a headstone, but was instead used as a footstone and never lettered.

Figure 50. Elias Carrington, 1800, Milford. Attributed to David Ritter.

Figure 51. Sally Ives, 1801, and Mariah Ives, 1795, New Haven. Decoration attributed to Thomas Gold. Lettering attributed to David Ritter.

Figure 52. Headstone used as footstone for Mehetabel [last name illegible], 1790, New Haven.

The stone for the Ives children is not the only one decorated by Gold and then inscribed by Ritter. In the East Side Cemetery at Woodbridge, for example, is a handsome slate, decorated with an urn and swag, inscribed for Amadeus Newton, who died in 1799 (figure 53); another, just like it, inscribed for William Hart and also dated 1799, is in the Central Cemetery in Wallingford. The lettering on each is in Ritter's characteristic style, and makes such a harmonious combination with the tympanum decoration that one might suppose that Ritter carved the whole. But if one compares other urns by Ritter (figure 50) with those by Gold (figure 46), the differences become apparent. Ritter's urns are squatter and less three-dimensional; they have a differently shaped base, and usually lack sprouts of willow at the sides, or coiled, ribbonlike swags around the shoulder. Also, the flower blossoms on Ritter's swags have only one set of petals, whereas Gold's always have two concentric sets. Almost without question, the Newton and Hart stones were decorated by Gold, and were part of the inventory purchased by Ritter for "recycling" (see Table 2, p. 55 and Appendix B).

Figure 53. Amadeus Newton, 1799, Woodbridge. Decoration attributed to Thomas Gold. Lettering attributed to David Ritter.

Figure 54. Thomas Gold, 1800. Decoration attributed to Thomas Gold. Lettering attributed to David Ritter. Signed by David Ritter.

Finally, there are the stones for Gold himself (figure 54) and for his wife, who outlived him by only a couple of months. Both are of eroded marble -- Anne Gold's has become almost illegible. Ritter actually signed the marker for Thomas Gold. But again, close examination of the tympanum urns, despite their poor condition, reveals that they are not by Ritter, but by Gold.

Conclusion

If for no other reason, the very size of Thomas Gold's output would make him a significant figure in the history of American gravestone carving. Without question, he was the most heavily patronized carver in his area, particularly in the period from the end of the Revolution to 1800. Moreover, his work documents important shifts in popular taste, as traditional dark sandstone gradually gave way to lighter-colored slate and marble, and the traditional soul effigy was supplanted by neoclassic imagery such as the cinerary urn.

But Gold's work deserves attention on aesthetic grounds as well. Provincial Connecticut gravestones of the last decades of the 18th century are sometimes rather casually dismissed, not only when measured against stones produced in cosmopolitan centers such as Boston and Newport, but also when compared with stones by carvers of earlier generations. But the work of Gold makes this judgment seem overly severe. His style is unquestionably spare and economical, sacrificing intricacy of workmanship to simplicity and ease of execution. The same can be said of much "country" furniture, architecture, and other arts of the period. It may result, as we have suggested earlier, more from economic limitations than lack of skill or talent. But other criteria are perhaps just as important: coherence and harmony of design, mastery of craftsmanship, refinement of taste, and individuality of style. Measured by these standards, Gold's work has considerable merit. We hope that this survey will awaken interest in an artist hitherto largely overlooked.

Table 1. Locations and periods of stones

	<-- SANDSTONE -->							Total Gold Stones	Derby Carver
	Up to 1777	Backdated Before 1782	1782-1789	1790-1800	Fragments (not dateable)	Marble	Slate		
Bethany	0	1	3	9	1	4	4	22	0
Bethel	2	2	2	0	0	2	0	8	0
Branford	0	2	2	5	2	1	2	14	0
Cheshire	0	0	0	3	1	0	4	8	5
Danbury	4	3	2	0	0	2	0	11	0
Derby	0	0	4	5	1	3	1	14	6
East Haven	2	1	11	16	4	1	1	36	3
Fairfield	0	3	4	0	0	0	0	7	4
Guilford	0	1	1	1	0	0	0	3	0
Madison	0	0	0	2	0	0	0	2	0
Meriden	1	0	1	0	1	0	0	3	1
Milford	0	5	14	9	2	2	21	53	1
New Haven	15	16	38	59	15	26	29	198	8
Newtown	0	8	3	0	0	6	1	18	0
North Haven	1	1	8	13	0	1	3	27	6
Northford	1	2	9	8	1	1	3	25	4
Redding	8	0	0	0	0	2	0	10	2
Seymour	0	0	2	1	0	5	5	13	0
Shelton	0	2	4	0	0	10	0	16	0
Stratford	20	10	15	0	2	0	1	48	2
Wallingford	4	0	0	1	1	0	3	9	2
West Haven	0	6	4	9	0	0	9	28	1
Woodbridge	2	3	14	11	3	2	17	52	0
Woodbury & Southbury	0	2	4	1	0	3	0	10	0
New York Suffolk County	0	4	4	2	0	0	0	10	0
Metropolitan area	0	0	0	0	0	0	0	0	3
Totals	60	72	149	155	34	71	104	645	48

Explanation of Table 1

The first category is made up of stones in both of Gold's prewar styles. All are sandstones, and none bears a date after 1777.

The second category is of sandstones that bear dates earlier than 1782, but are in Gold's postwar style, and presumably backdated.

The next two categories cover the rest of Gold's postwar sandstones, from 1782 to 1800. Some of those bearing dates in the 1780s are probably back-dated, but precise stylistic distinctions between works of the 1780s and 1790s are hard to make.

The undateable sandstone fragments not only lack dates, but are in such poor condition that they cannot be dated by style.

The marbles are all in Gold's postwar style. Most appear to be works of the 1790s.

The slates are all clearly works of the 1790s.

The stones attributed to the Derby Carver bear dates from 1773 to 1778. Only those of the mid-1770s have borders in the styles of Gold or Baldwin, or display other evidence of collaboration with Gold.

Table 2. Neoclassic (urn design) stones attributed to Gold

	Sandstone	Marble	Slate
Bethany	0	0	1
East Haven	1	0	0
New Haven	1	7*	2
Newtown	0	1*	0
Northford	0	0	1*
Wallingford	0	0	1*
West Haven	1	0	0
Woodbridge	0	0	2*
Totals	3	8	7

* Includes one lettered by David Ritter.

Appendix A

Probate records of payments to Thomas Gold, from the notes of Ernest Caulfield, a copy of which is in possession of the authors. Amounts are in pounds, shillings, and pence. The present locations of the stones are referred to when known.

David Lattin, paid 1750: "To Mr. Gold" 0-14-6.
(Stratford; stone not found. Also recorded is a payment of 1-6-6 "To Wm Lampson"; the Lamsons were wellknown carvers in the Boston area. Payment to "Mr. Gold" may have been for erecting the stone, or a fee to Thomas Gold's father, the Rev. Hezekiah Gold, for conducting the funeral.)

Kate Leavitt, paid 1760: "To Thomas Gold" 3-19-6.
(Fairfield; stone not found. A rather mysterious record, since there is no evidence of any Gold stones carved so early.)

Abner Judson, died 1774, paid 1775: "Paid to Thomas Gold for grave stones" 3-18-0.
(Old Burying Ground, Stratford. Red sandstone, soul-effigy design. The first existing stone for which there is a probate record.)

John Brooks, died 1777, paid 1788: "To Tomas Gould for Grave Stones" 3-6-0.
(Old Burying Ground, Stratford. Red sandstone, soul-effigy design. The stone appears to have been carved in 1777, and paid for later.)

Edward Hawley, paid 1782: "To Cash paid Mr Thomas Gould for Grave Stones" 2-2-0.
(Old Burying Ground, Stratford. Red sandstone, soul-effigy design.)

Samuel Willcockson ("Wilcoxson" in probate records), paid 1783: "Thomas Gold for tomb Stons" 3-4-0.
(Old Burying Ground, Stratford. Red sandstone, soul-effigy design.)

Benajah Peck, died 1785, paid 1787: "To Mr Gold for Grave Stones" 5-0-0.
(Old Cemetery, Meyers Road, Bethany. Badly worn marble, soul-effigy design.)

Chauncey Whittelsey, paid 1787: "Thos. Gould" 8-2-0.
(Crypt of Center Church, New Haven. Marble, soul-effigy design.)

John Tappen ("Tapping" in probate records), died 1793, paid 1794: "Nov 2 To Mr Goold for grave stones" 1-16-0.
(Grove Street Cemetery, New Haven. Red sandstone, soul-effigy design.)

Jonathan Fitch, died 1793, paid 1795: "Decr. 1 To paid for Grave Stones to Thos Gould" 7-16-0.
(New Haven; stone not found.)

Joseph Humaston, paid 1795: "To Mr Gould for gravestones" 1-19-0.

(Hamden Plains Cemetery, New Haven. Red sandstone, broken and mostly illegible.)

Andrew Smith, paid 1796: "To Thomas Gold" 2-14-0.
(New Haven; stone not found.)

John Smith, paid 1796: "To Cash paid Mr Thomas Gold for Grave Stones" 9-0-0.
(New Haven; stone not found.)

Stephen Trowbridge, paid 1796: "To Cash pd Thomas Gould for Grave-Stones" 2-8-0.
(Crypt of Center Church, New Haven. Red sandstone, soul-effigy design.)

Mary Merwin, died 1797, paid 1799: "Thos Gold to one pare of grave Stones" 3-0-0.
(Milford Cemetery. Slate, soul-effigy design.)

Thomas Mansfield, died 1798, paid 1800: "To Mr Thomas Gould for two sets of Grave Stones" 7-7-0.
(North Haven. Thomas Mansfield stone is noted by Caulfield as broken, and is now missing, but stone for Hannah Mansfield [died 1798], possibly his wife, remains. Red sandstone, soul-effigy design.)

Deacon James Gilbert, died 1798, paid 1800: "Feb 27 1800 to paying Mr Goold for Grave Stones" 4-10-0.
(Grove Street Cemetery, New Haven. Slate, urn design. Caulfield comments, "Must have been his *last* -- died March 1800.")

Appendix B

Stones with decoration attributed to Thomas Gold, and lettering attributed to David Ritter.

Lydie Atwater, 1784, New Haven.
(Red sandstone, soul effigy design.)

Jabez Backus, 1794, New Haven.
(Marble, urn design.)

Sally Ives, 1801, and Mariah Ives, 1795, New Haven.
(Slate, soul effigy design.)

Thomas Gold, 1800, New Haven.
(Marble, urn design. Signed by Ritter. Appears to be one of a pair, along with stone for wife Anne Gold.)

Anne Gold, 1800, Newtown.
(Marble, urn design.)

Isaac Foot, 1799, Northford.
(Slate, urn design.)

Matthew Dick, 1801, Wallingford.
(Slate, urn design. Appears to be one of a pair, along with stone for Amadeus Newton.)

Amadeus Newton, 1799, Woodbridge.
(Slate, urn design.)

NOTES

1. Morris W. Abbott, *Old Tombstones in Milford Cemetery, or Styles in Steles*, (Milford, Connecticut: 1974).
2. David J. Corrigan, "Symbols and Carvers of New England Gravestones," *Journal of the New Haven Colony Historical Society*, Spring 1976 Vol. 25 no. 1 (New Haven: New Haven Colony Historical Society), p. 13.
3. Letters from David Corrigan to Richard F. Welch, April 30 and May 31, 1982. Richard F. Welch, *Memento Mori: The Gravestones of Early Long Island* (Syosset, New York: Friends for Long Island's Heritage, 1983), p. 60.
4. Ernest Caulfield, unpublished notes and writings, in the possession of James A. Slater, Mansfield Center, Connecticut.
5. Corrigan, "Symbols and Carvers," p. 13.
6. Donald Lines Jacobus, *History and Genealogy of the Families of Old Fairfield*, Vol. II (New Haven: Tuttle Morehouse and Taylor & Co., 1932), p. 53.
7. Corrigan, "Symbols and Carvers," p. 13.
8. Letter from Corrigan to Welch, April 30, 1982.
9. Ibid.
10. Williston Walker, "The Sandemanians of New England," *Annual Report for the American Historical Association, 1901* (Washington, D.C.: U.S. Government Printing Office, 1902), p. 137.
11. Ibid, p. 144.
12. Advertisement, *Connecticut Journal* (New Haven, March 5, 1773), p.1.
13. Walker, "The Sandemanians," p. 156.
14. From Ezra Stiles manuscripts, quoted in Walker, "The Sandemanians," footnote p. 155.
15. New Haven Land Records, Vol. 34, p. 508.
16. Franklin Bowditch Dexter, *Biographical Sketches of the Graduates of Yale College*, Vol. 3 (New York: Henry Holt and Company, 1903), p. 107.
17. List of probated stones from Caulfield's notes. Reproduced in Appendix A.
18. Caulfield, unpublished notes on Michael Baldwin.
19. New Haven Colony Historical Society, *History of the City of New Haven to the Present Time* (New Haven: New Haven Colony Historical Society), p. 532.
20. From Ezra Stiles manuscripts, quoted in Walker, "The Sandemanians," footnote p. 155.
21. New Haven Land Records, Vol. 43, p. 173.
22. Ibid., Vol. 44, p. 81.
23. Probate inventory, recorded April 1, 1800.
24. New Haven Land Records, Vol. 44, p. 81.
25. Elizabeth Mills Brown, *New Haven: A Guide to Architecture and Urban Design* (New Haven: Yale University Press, 1976), p. 197.
26. New Haven Land Records, Vol. 48, p. 53.
27. Probate record, recorded April 1, 1800. Gold's gravestone in Grove Street Cemetery, which

       records his age at death as 68, is incorrect.
28. Gravestone in Newtown Cemetery.
29. 1790 Census Report for New Haven County, p. 103.
30. New Haven Land Records, Vol. 35, p. 128.
31. Walker, "The Sandemanians," p. 156-157.
32. For example, Corrigan, "Symbols and Carvers," p. 13; Welch, *Memento Mori*, p. 59-60.
33. Caulfield, unpublished notes. Also gravestone of Anne Gold, Newtown.
34. Probate inventory, recorded April 1, 1800.
35. New Haven Land Records, Vol. 53, p. 409.

Acknowledgements

Much of the background material for this article comes not from published sources, but directly from individuals. We are deeply grateful to the following members of the Association for Gravestone Studies, who were unstintingly generous in providing information and advice.

Alice Bunton, of Bethany, Connecticut, for information on the graveyards of New Haven County and of eastern Fairfield County.

Daniel and Jessie Lie Farber, of Worcester, Massachusetts, for providing photographs from their collection, and for further information on Gold stones which they have recorded.

Laurel Gabel, for photocopies of photographs in the Farber Collection, and for references to the Connecticut researchers listed here.

Jim Halpin of Wallingford, Connecticut, for information on the graveyards of New Haven County, particularly Wallingford and East Haven.

Daniel Allen Hearn of Monroe, Connecticut, for information on the graveyards of central Fairfield County, particularly Danbury, Redding, and Newtown.

Miriam Silverman, Curator of Trinity Parish, New York City, for information on the stones in Trinity and St. Paul churchyards.

James Slater of Mansfield, Connecticut, for information on the Connecticut Valley carving tradition and the Ritter family. Also for copies of the unpublished notes on Gold and Michael Baldwin by the late Ernest Caulfield.

Richard Welch, of Huntington, New York, for information on the graveyards of Long Island and the New York metropolitan area, and for photographs of stones in these graveyards.

Anne Williams and Sue Kelly, respectively of Darien and Stamford, Connecticut, for information on the graveyards in Fairfield and New Haven Counties, particularly the shore communities; and for permission to reproduce their elegant rubbing of the signed Caleb Hotchkiss stone, 1779.

Also, we should like to thank Margaret Wixstead of Redding, Connecticut, for information on the graveyards of Redding.

Finally, special thanks are due to Abbott L. Cummings of Yale University, for his suggestions and criticisms of the thesis by Meredith Williams on which this article is based.

Fig. 1. St. John - Hill United Church of Christ, Berks County.
(All photographs by the author.)

PENNSYLVANIA GERMAN GRAVESTONES: AN INTRODUCTION

Thomas E. Graves

Starting with the arrival of the ship Concord on October 6, 1683, a flood of immigrants from Germany, Switzerland and parts of France began which would continue until the American Revolution.[1] Some of these people settled in Germantown, others fanned out in an arc surrounding Philadelphia which extended from what is now western Bucks to northern Chester Counties. The religious affiliations of these immigrants were varied, but can be classed into three main groups: the church groups, mainly Lutherans and Reformed (the latter now part of the United Church of Christ); the sectarian groups, the so-called plain people including the Amish and Mennonites; and, numerically the smallest, the communitarians, such as the society at Ephrata.[2] A second wave of German immigration began in the 1830s and continued through most of the century. This wave was even less homogenous than the first. These later immigrants mixed with the earlier ones only to a certain extent, with a greater percentage settling in urban areas or continuing to the midwest. Because of the differences in time, continental origins, and settlement patterns, one of the accepted definitions of "the Pennsylvania Germans" includes only those who came in the first wave of migration and their descendants, including those who moved from Pennsylvania into Ohio, Maryland, Ontario, or other regions.[3]

This paper will discuss the evolution of the gravestones found in the graveyards of the church groups of Berks, Lancaster, Lebanon, Schuylkill, Lehigh and Montgomery Counties (Maps 1 and 2). These counties have the major historical settlements of Lutheran and Reformed Pennsylvania Germans. The earliest stones in this rural region date from the 1740s, sixty years after the start of the German immigration.[4] These stones are among the earliest surviving examples of Pennsylvania German gravestones because some of the oldest graveyards in Germantown and other urban areas have given way to urban construction.[5] Another reason for the lack of very early markers is that the earliest markers may have been made out of wood. Also, the earliest immigrants were the Mennonites.[6] The Lutheran and Reformed congregations were formed later. Lutherans were living in

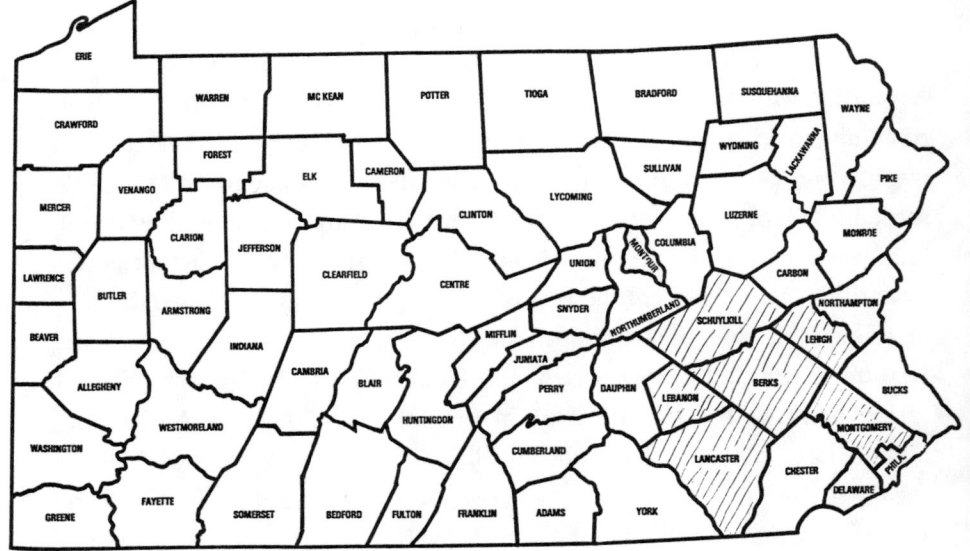

Map 1. The Pennsylvania Counties included in this study

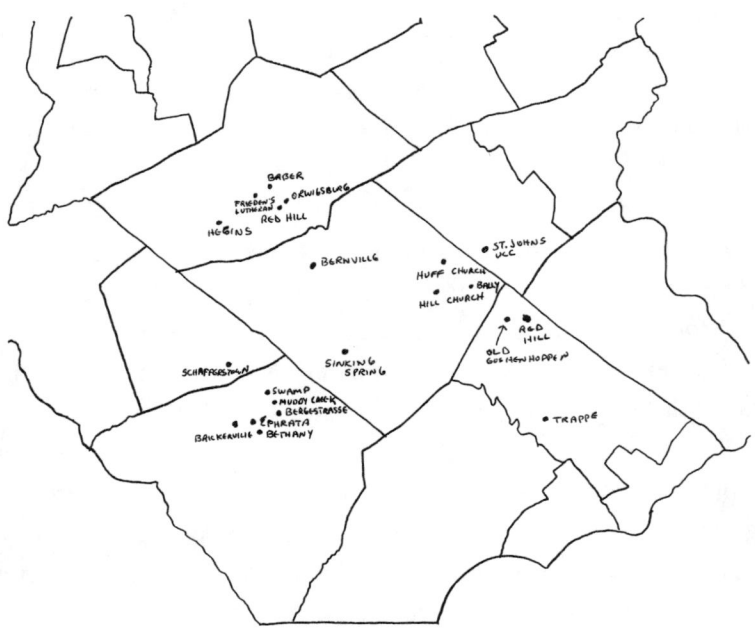

Map 2. Graveyards visited for this study

Germantown before 1700. The Lutheran (1717) and Reformed (1725) congregations, formed at Falkner Swamp, also known as New Hanover, in Montgomery County, are among the earliest congregations for these denominations in this country.[7] Few pre-revolutionary stones remain in the yard of the old Trappe Lutheran Church which was built in 1743. Brickerville Lutheran Church in Lancaster County was formed in 1730, Hill Union Church in Berks County in 1731 (Fig. 1), Muddy Creek Union Church in Lancaster County in 1732.[8] Because of the size of this region, the focus of the discussion will be on broad cultural trends, leaving out those which occurred within a single community or congregation.

The earliest stones in many cemeteries are often the plainest with poorly executed decoration and text, but such stones may be found with later dates if the families could not afford better (Fig. 2). In many graveyards, however, the fieldstone and roughly executed markers disappear by 1800. A small, roughly lettered sandstone marker with no decoration from the graveyard of Zion Lutheran "Red" Church in Orwigsburg, Schuylkill County, for example, has simply:

   Iacob . Weis   Jacob Weis
   Den (7?) Nofember   The (7th?) November
   1795   1795

Note the phonetic spelling of "November." One of the earliest dated stones at the Muddy Creek Lutheran Church graveyard is a small stone with a rough "flat heart" (a heart based on circles) with no downwards indentation at the top. Inside this heart are the initials "C E L." Over the heart is the date 1757.

Often these "primitive" stones are shaped like the fancier ones but have crude lettering; others are finely executed but are small and have minimal information carved on them. On some graves the headstone is missing, leaving just the footstone. These footstones must not be confused with plain or primitive headstones. In Eastern Lebanon County wrought iron crosses were used occasionally during the second half of the nineteenth century.[9] Wooden markers have also been used, but most of these have decayed and disappeared. Two wooden markers were still extant at St. Jacob's

Fig. 2. This marker starts with a stark "HIER LEGT BEGRABEN" (Here lies buried). In the arch is a tulip, one of the most popular of the folk motifs, and the date "1746." Above the date are the letters "G" and "B." These letters probably stand for *gebornen* (born): this person, Andereas Herb, was born in 1746. He was 13 years, 8 months, and 20 days old when he died. He awaits the resurrection of his saviour Jesus Christ (UND WARDET DER AUFERSTEUNG SEINES ERLOESERS JESUS CHRISTI). The last line we can see above ground says "GESTORBEN DN 23..." (He died the 23rd). The top of the death date (1759) can just be seen on the next line. St. John - Hill United Church of Christ, Berks County.

(Kimmerling's) Church in Lebanon County when McDonald did his study of Lebanon County gravestones in 1975.[10] Any inscription which might have been on these stones has long since weathered away. They were upright boards with the tops cut to follow the style of stone markers. Lewis Miller made a drawing of the York, Pennsylvania, Potters Field in 1808. In this drawing there are many crosses which were probably made of wood.[11] A few wooden crosses are still standing in the Bally, Pennsylvania, Catholic graveyard.

The most conservative element on Pennsylvania German gravestones is the textual material which forms the epitaph carved on the face. Typical is the epitaph on this child's stone:

Hier	Here
ruhet im Gott	rests in God
Maria Wrenerin	Maria Wren
Ist Geboren den 14ien	Born the 14th
October, 1790 Starb	of October, 1790 Died
den 19ien July, 1794	the 19th of July, 1794

(Hill Church, Berks County)

The phrase *im Gott* does not always appear; however, the rest of the inscription is the basic text format for epitaphs on Pennsylvania German stones into the early twentieth century. The birth date is as important as the death date and is rarely omitted. The carvers recreated in stone the German lettering used in German language publications and on fraktur, the Pennsylvania German illuminated manuscripts. At least one of these carvers, Daniel Peterman of York County, 1797-1871, was also a schoolteacher who produced fraktur.[12]

To the biographical kernel, additional information was often added.

Hier ruhet	Here rests
Samuel J. Dondore	Samuel J. Dondore
Eatte den	Husband to
Maria Eine geborne	Maria who was born
Strauss	Strauss
Geb. den 5 Marz	Born on the 5th of March
1845	1845
Starb den 18 Decem.	Died the 18th of December
1870	1870
Alt 25 Jahr 9 Mon., 13 T.	Aged 25 years, 9 months, 13 days

Text Jesaias 60 V 20.   Text Isaiah chapter 60, verse 20.
(Bernville, Berks County)

Fig. 3. This stone for Susan Seipel is a mid-nineteenth century example of use of the rosette, or "hex sign" motif. The epitaph starts with "ZUM AN-DENKEN AN" (To the memory of). She was born (her maiden name was) Bhom and was the wife of John Seipel. She was born the 8th of July, 1813. She lived in marriage 9 years and 4 months and had 3 children and died the 22nd of February, 1844 aged 30 years, 6 months, and 25 days. St. Paul's Union Church, Trexlertown, Lehigh County.

Often the person's age will be spelled out to the day. The "spousal" or "family" biography names the husband or wife and usually one or more of the following items: the wife's maiden name, the year the couple was married, the number of children, the number of children of each sex, and the number of grandchildren (Fig. 3). Any children who died before the parent and were buried in the same family plot may be listed or mentioned, but this is not common. If the person was unmarried, the stone sometimes names the parents. Frederick S. Weiser, in his article discussing the relationship between the artistic genres of birth and death and their importance to the Pennsylvania Germans, points out that this form of biography is also found on Pennsylvania German *Geburts- und Taufscheine* (birth and baptismal certificates).[13] In at least one case the same text is contained on both the birth and baptismal certificate and the gravestone. Weiser calls the biographical epitaph typical, but in the geographical region examined in this study the extended biographical epitaphs appear only on a quarter to a third of the stones. A further connection between *Taufscheine* and tombstones is that some families would add the death dates, and sometimes the marriage dates, to the baptismal certificate.[14]

Verses, sayings, and hymns forming part of the epitaph are generally rare on Pennsylvania German gravestones. There are, however, micro-regions, consisting of one or more graveyards, such as St. Paul's Union Church near Trexlertown, where this form is more abundant. If there is anything in addition to biographical data, there may be the biblical reference for the sermon given at the funeral service. Although it is more common in these cases to head the biblical reference with *Text*, some stones have *Leichen Text* (funeral text). In the Brickerville Lutheran churchyard the term *Leichen Text* occurs frequently.

Denkmal	Memorial
für	for
Aaron Nester,	Aaron Nester,
Sohn von	Son of
Daniel u. Esther	Daniel and Esther
Nester.	Nester.
Er war geboren den 22.	He was born the 22nd of
Juni 1825. Starb den 14.	June, 1825. He died the 14th of
Sept. 1857: war alt 32	September, 1857: He was aged 32

Jahre, 2 Mon. und.	Years, 2 Months and
22 Tage.	22 Days.
Leichen Text: I Cor. 15, 31.	Funeral Text: I Cor. 15, 31
Ich Sterbe täglich.	I die daily.
(Hill Church, Berks County)	

In Samuel Dondore's epitaph, quoted above, the reference is to a verse from Isaiah which, in the King James version, reads:

Thy sun shall no more go down,
neither thy moon withdraw itself:
for the Lord shall be thine everlasting light,
and the days of thy mourning shall be ended.

If a verse does appear, it is usually the first line of the listed Bible reference, as on the stone for Aaron Nester, above, or on the stone for William Faust, whose funeral sermon was based on Job 7, verse 16: "I would not live always." Sometimes the hymns used at the funeral service are also listed.[15]

Henry Nester	Henry Nester
Geboren Aug. 20. 1817	Born August 20, 1817
Starb July 28. 1892	Died July 28, 1892
Alt	Aged
74 Jahre. 11 mo.	74 Years, 11 Months
8 Tage.	8 Days.

(The following lines are inscribed in the open Bible above Henry Nester's Name)

Text: Johan 14. 19.	Text: John 14. 19.
Lieder No. 153. 167.	Hymns No. 153. 167.
(Hill Church, Berks County)	

The form of epitaph considered thus far is found consistently from colonial times to the early twentieth century. A different form of biography, giving the details of immigration, was sometimes used in the late eighteenth and early nineteenth centuries among the Pennsylvania Germans. Here we have the epitaph for a Swiss woman (Fig. 4):

Fig. 4. An undecorated stone from the graveyard adjoining the Ephrata Cloisters in Lancaster County. Elisabeth Keller immigrated here from Switzerland and joined the cloisters. She died in 1787.

Hier ruhet	Here rests
ein Glied der	a member of the
Gemeindein Ephrata	Ephrata community,
Elisabeth Kellern	Elisabeth Keller
Gebornen im hof, von	Born in the town of
Wintersingen	Wintersingen
im Canton, Basel.	in Canton Basel.
Geboren Feb. 2.1708	Born February 2, 1708.
Starb May 24.1787.	Died May 24, 1787.
Alter 79 Jahre, 3 monate	Aged 79 years, 3 months
und 22 Tage.	and 22 days.

(Ephrata, Lancaster County)

The features of an immigrant biography include the immigrant's place of birth and sometimes, although not here, the year of immigration. This form of gravestone biography was used among the English-speaking population during the same period.

Pennsylvania German fashion paralleled English tastes in the nineteenth century in many areas, including, for example, the design and ornamentation of furniture and domestic architecture. Most of the eighteenth-century Pennsylvania German epitaphs begin *Hier ruhet* (Here rests). Other early stones begin *Hier Legt* (Here Lies). These headings last in some areas into the 1870s. Beginning in the first decade of the nineteenth century, the forms *Zum Andenken an* (To the Memory of) and *Denkmal für* (A memorial for) were used and became more common as the century wore on. This change follows a trend seen in English language gravestones away from concern with the physical remains of the dead person toward the memory of that person -- a "cult of the memorial", what Ariès calls the age of the "death of the other."[16]

Zum Andenken an	To the memory of
Abraham Yoder	Abraham Yoder
Sohn von	Son of
George u. Maria	George and Maria
Yoder,	Yoder
Geboren d.12.Dec.1785:	Born the 12th of December, 1785:
Verheirathete sich mir	He married
Elisabeth Yerger.	Elisabeth Yerger
Den 21 Mai.1809. Zengien	on the 21st of May,1809.
	They begot
5 Sohne und 6 Tochter.	5 sons and 6 daughters.
Starb den 5.April 1864.	Died the 5th of April, 1864.

Alt 78 Jahre, 5 Mo.   Aged 78 years, 5 months,
und 23 Tage.   and 23 days.
   (Hill Church, Berks County) (Fig. 5)

Fig. 5. The marker for Abraham Yoder (d. 1864) has a complete biography of his married life. See text for translation. St. John - Hill United Church of Christ, Berks County.

While the heading has changed from "Here Rests" to "To the Memory of," the format of the epitaph remains unchanged. The particulars of who the person was continue to be more important than how those particulars are presented.

Unlike the major part of the epitaph, the decorative carving on Pennsylvania German gravestones have continued to change and evolve into the twentieth century. Two sets of patterns have influenced each other while retaining their own flavor. The first form of decoration is derived from current high fashion of the period. Such forms as death's heads, skulls, and hour glasses appear on highly sculptured stones shaped and influenced by German baroque and rococo forms and design. The explicit death motifs are not common, but they stand out prominently among the other stones. Some of these early stones have decoration on both sides. Others use the reverse side of the stone for the placement of the religious text. Both Barba and Lichten illustrate gravestones from the German Palatinate which represent the kinds of stones with which the early immigrants would be familiar.[17] Included on both the Palatinate and the early Pennsylvania German stones are ornate floral designs deriving from elite fashion rather than from the folk art floral motifs (Fig. 6). The majority of early Pennsylvania German stones are often made from red sandstone and are usually five to seven inches thick. The baroque forms give way to neo-classical ones as death's heads evolve into cherubs and angels (Fig. 7). The cherub motif was used into the mid-nineteenth century. Portraits are rare.

The other decorative tradition relies on the motifs of Pennsylvania German folk art. Among the most mysterious of Pennsylvania German gravestones are elaborately decorated stones with no textual material (Fig. 8). Most of these stones are decorated on both sides. They are found in Lancaster County graveyards and have been mentioned by several early writers on Pennsylvania German folk art, often without comment. No one has ever discovered why they have no text or whose graves they mark. Preston A. Barba believes that these stones all had inscriptions but that they were so lightly inscribed that the epitaphs have weathered away.[18] A close inspection of the markers (usually of sandstone) reveals that the ornamentation is deeply cut and that on most of them the unmarked areas are smooth with

Fig. 6. Flowers on eighteenth-century Pennsylvania German gravestones were living, flowing, and climbing plants. In the mid-1800s, the Victorian convention of cut flowers became popular. At the bottom of the marker, it states that the funeral text was taken from 1 Corinthians, verses 15 and 31, "I die daily" (Leichen-Text: 1 Cor. 15,31. Ich sterbe täglich). St. John - Hill United Church of Christ, Berks County.

no uneven weathering. However, at the Muddy Creek churchyard there are some stones which appear to have been carved by the same person and which do have deeply cut decoration with the faintest remains of an epitaph. Another carver, for whom the moon was a favorite motif, carved stones which still have easily readable texts. Some of the stones at Muddy Creek appear to be by the same carvers as those without epitaphs but have a name, deeply cut and usually consisting of the first initial and the surname. John Joseph Stoudt has several examples of these stones but comments only on their "interesting designs" without discussing their lack of text.[19] Francis Lichten, one of the early writers on Pennsylvania German folk art, illustrates these stones, like Stoudt, without comment.[20]

Were these markers without epitaphs once painted? Did they mark the graves of suicide victims? Or were they carver's samples? All three theories have been raised, but we simply do not know the answer, although the first explanation seems the most likely.[21] There are simply too many of

Fig. 7. A cherub with various fruits, including grapes and an apple. Pre-1800, but the date is sunk into the ground. St. John - Hill United Church of Christ, Berks County.

Fig. 8. A carved stone without any text from Bergestrasse Lutheran Church, Lancaster County. The portrait is bordered by tulips and tulips sprout from the columns on the side. Date unknown.

these stones to have served merely as samples or to have marked suicides. Some graveyards, such as that at the Bergestrasse Lutheran Church, have only a few of these stones. Muddy Creek churchyard has about two dozen, with a majority of the pre-1800 full-sized sandstone markers without text. In Germany some forms of markers were painted, such as those of wrought iron and those placed inside the church. German wooden markers, at least in the nineteenth century, had both painted decorations and epitaphs. Did the tradition of painted markers in Germany date back far enough and did it exist in the Palatinate early enough to influence the early immigrants to Pennsylvania?[22] Further research into German scholarship or fieldwork in German graveyards might supply the answers.

Among the more popular folk art motifs on these stones are "trees of life" (*Lebensbaum*), hearts, suns, moons, and stars. Several scholars of Pennsylvania German folklore and religion have theorized on the possible meaning of these motifs. Stoudt maintains throughout all of his works on Pennsylvania German folklore and folk art that the tree of life, which may have lilies, roses, or tulips, is a Christian expression of the joy of religious life and salvation.[23] He bases his conclusion on, among other reasons, the occurrence of biblical and religious verses appearing with these motifs on fraktur and illumination. Among the verses he finds are ones from the Song of Songs and the Sermon on the Mount. Louis Winkler, in his gravestone installment in a series of articles on Pennsylvania German astronomy and astrology, points out that the moon is most often shown with the cusps pointing either to the right or downwards. These moons are shown to be waning, "on the decrease," and therefore appropriate, in Winkler's view, for gravestones.[24] He notes that the half-sun found on some of the stones is ambiguous, for it could be interpreted as either a rising or setting sun. Some stones have arcs, either alone or with other motifs such as a heart or a tree of life. Barba, in what is still the only volume devoted solely to Pennsylvania German gravestones, interprets these arcs as representations of the Germanic *Ur-bogen*, the descending arc of the sun at the time of the winter solstice.[25] The winter solstice is a time of death and rebirth, the old sun dies and the new one is born (Fig. 9).

Fig. 9. A carved stone filled with astronomical symbols but completely lacking in text. The moon is pointing downwards and slightly to the right, representing the waning moon. Bergestrasse Lutheran Church, Lancaster County. Date unknown.

Flowers, similar to those found on fraktur, often appear. Flat hearts are sometimes seen. Swirling, or curvilinear, swastikas are found. Barba sees this motif as representing good luck and a means of warding off evil, but he does not give a specific interpretation of its use on gravestones.[26]

Stars and rosettes, designs found on Pennsylvania German barns and today called "hex signs," are common in some graveyards, almost nonexistent in others.[27] These motifs also vary with time, being found on eighteenth-century stones in some cemeteries, such as Brickerville, and on nineteenth-century stones in others, such as the "Red Church" in Orwigsburg. Ludwig interpreted rosettes as soul effigies.[28] Rosettes are found on gravestones in most European countries and on stones and monuments going back many centuries. Objects with rosettes on them have been buried with the dead since at least the time of Mycenean Greece (1200-1500 BC). Before their use as "grave goods," these objects were diadems, pendants, and scales.[29] The rosette has had many other meanings and associations over the centuries, especially among the Germanic peoples, who have called the rosette a *Glükstern* (lucky star) or *Glückrad* (lucky wheel). The six-pointed star was the symbol of "Frau Sonne" and "Frau Fortuna." As Lady Fortune, operating the ever present wheel of fortune, the rosette (Fig. 3) is an appropriate motif for a gravestone, readily associated with the familiar *memento mori* device.[30]

The rosette also has ethnic connotations. Among the Pennsylvania Germans the rosette is often found with other Pennsylvania German motifs such as the flat heart and stylized flowers. An increase in the use of rosettes occurred in the 1840s and 1850s, at a time when the German culture and language were under attack by the state of Pennsylvania. Templates with the rosette were popular during the first half of the twentieth century among both Protestants and Catholics. These templates illustrate the use of an ethnic identity marker in a mass produced item, the cemetery marker. These markers were selected by the relatives and then filled in with the deceased person's name and his birth and death dates. The context in which rosettes are found on Pennsylvania German gravestones suggests that this motif may have been used as an ethnic marker.[31]

Fig. 10. The willow was used throughout the nineteenth century among the Pennsylvania Germans, including the Mennonites. The epitaph reads "Here rests Peter Lang. Son of George and Elisabeth Lang. Born the 27th of February, 1792. Died the 30th of August, 1863. Aged 71 years, 6 months and 3 days." The carver's initials, "C.H.L.," appear in the lower right hand corner. C.H. Lautenbach of Schuylkill Haven was active in Southern Schuylkill County for several decades in the mid-1800s. Zion Lutheran "Red" Church, Orwigsburg, Schuylkill County.

The decorations used on Pennsylvania German stones changed with the times, while the textual format and content remained the same. Thus in the nineteenth century Pennsylvania Germans adopted all the popular gravestone designs. This is another area in which the Pennsylvania German fashions were influenced by English ones. But what was said about the dead remained constant. Willows appear shortly after 1800 and are found frequently through the 1860s and occasionally up to the end of the century (Fig. 10). Doves are common from the mid-century. Flowers, always popular among the Pennsylvania Germans, take many forms during the last half-century, both in arrangement and as individual flowers, including the rose, tulip, and the lily-of-the-valley. These flowers are often cut flowers, denoting a life cut off in the bud (Fig. 6). A wilted cut flower was sometimes used for emphasis.[32] Eighteenth-century flowers on Pennsylvania German stones were more often growing vines resembling the common "tree-of-life" motif, although the "tree of life" reappeared at about the same time as the revival of the rosette. Wreaths, often used with Bibles, were popular at mid-century. Other motifs include the upraised hand, open Bibles, churches, pomengranates, and monuments which enclose the space of the grave. Open Bibles often contain the funeral sermon and hymn references. Angels often appear on mid-century stones. Sometimes the angel carries a little figure in its arms (Fig. 11). When the deceased is an elderly person, this tiny figure is obviously a soul effigy, as shown in prints of death-bed scenes from the same period.[33]

Photographs, either daguerreotypes or more modern processes, appear but rarely. Most of the early stones which had photographs mounted on them have lost the photographs, leaving a blank depression where they had been set. These deteriorated stones can be interpreted only if it is known that photographs had been used.

The Pennsylvania German Catholic community used the same textual format for their epitaphs and the same broad spectrum of motifs as the Protestants. However, a cross was usually added. The major Pennsylvania German Catholic graveyard, in Bally, Berks County, has the full spectrum of Victorian designs.

Fig. 11. An angel bearing a soul effigy of Mariah Erb, who was 78 years old when she died in 1896. The epitaph contains the basic kernel of text which was carried over from German into English during the nineteenth century. St. John - Hill United Church of Christ, Berks County.

The Pennsylvania Germans had their own version of the mid-century fashion of imitating typeset lettering. As with the equivalent English stones, several lettering styles, or fonts, were used on one stone. The fonts used on these stones, however, are an evolution of German script and type fonts rather than imitations of English typesetting styles.

Eventually English came to be used on Pennsylvania German gravestones. This change occurred at varying times for each community. At Bergestrasse Lutheran Church in Lancaster County, which has numerous elaborate eighteenth-century stones, the change occurred early, around 1820, after which there is little difference between this cemetery and any non-Pennsylvania German cemetery. At Orwigsburg's Red Church and at Muddy Creek German was used to some extent until about 1900. In a few places, such as Bernville in Berks County, the use of German predominates throughout the nineteenth century, with some examples as late as the 1930s. In many communities the change occurred shortly before or during the Civil War period.

The change in language did not mean a change in content. The epitaph continued to follow the same patterns outlined above.

> In Memory of
> Joseph
> Son of
> Daniel & Elizabeth
> Faust.
> Born July 30th, 1833.
> Died April 16, 1866.
> Aged 32 years 8 months &
> 17 days.
> Text Psalm 39 v 8 & 11.
>   (Zion Lutheran "Red" Church, Schuylkill County)

The spousal biography was also used in English.

> Sarah Ann
> Wife of
> Frederick L. Turpin
> Nee Freyberger.
> And mother of
> Andrew W. Turpin.
> Born Dec 15, 1848.
> Died March 17, 1870.

    Aged 21 years 8 M. 2D.
    Text Matth 24:44
        (Bernville, Berks County)

One of the early stones to appear in English was an adaptation of the immigrant's biography, the difference being that instead of Germany or Switzerland as the place of birth, the woman had immigrated from Lancaster to Schuylkill County. The epitaph includes a spousal biography.

    In
    Memory Of
    Susanna Kelley
    Daughter of Cyrus and
    Catherina Numan who was
    born in Numanstown
    Lancaster County
    Pennsylvania in the year
    1770 and departed this
    life the 2nd October, 1828
    in her 38th year. She was
    married on the 22nd
    of January, 1808.
    May the soul of the
    Departed rest in
    Peace.
        (Zion Lutheran "Red" Church, Schuylkill County)

It is interesting to note that both the place of Susanna Kelley's birth and death were later made parts of different counties. Numanstown became part of Lebanon County while Orwigsburg, in Berks County until 1811, became part of Schuylkill. We cannot tell from Susanna Kelley's epitaph if she migrated before or after the formation of Schuylkill County. Although we can glean important genealogical and historical information from gravestones, we cannot learn everything we should like to know.

The most common epitaph was still a verse used in the funeral sermon, but now it was rendered in English, as on this stone for Maria Young, who died in 1907:

    Maria Young
    Wife of
    Joseph J.R. Zerfass
    Born Sept. 3, 1843
    Died April 15, 1907

>
> Aged
> 63 Years, & Mos
> 12 Days
>
> 2 Timothy 4:7. I have fought
> a good fight, I have finished
> my course, I have kept the faith.
> (Ephrata, Lancaster County)

Once the epitaphs became rendered in English, more of the common English language phrases began to appear, such as "Gone but not Forgotten" on a stone for Daniel Boyer.

Funeral verses were rare in German epitaphs but were used more frequently in those rendered in English, such as this verse on Mary Beyerle's stone:

> In
> Memory of
> Mary,
> Wife of
> George Beyerle.
> was born May 22nd 1823.
> Died June 9th 1848
> Aged
> 26 Years & 14 Days
>
> Farewell dear Husband my life is past
> My love for you till death did last,
> And after me no sorrow take
> But love our children for my sake.
> (Bernville, Berks County)

The biographical portion remains with the appearance of these English epitaphs. The biblical reference used for the funeral service is often omitted, but sometimes both the reference and a verse appear, as on this stone for Lydia Matz (Fig. 12):

> Lydia
> Wife of
> John Matz
> And Daughter of
> P. & E. Fegly
> Born Nov. 1st 1814
> Died April 26th 1875
> Aged 60 Y. 5 M. & 25 D.

Text Psalm 23.1
_____

Remember friends when you pass by,
As you are now, so once was I.
As I am now, so you will be,
Prepare for death and follow me.
        (Zion Lutheran "Red" Church, Schuylkill County)

Fig. 12. The stone for Lydia Matz was carved by "C.L." (C.H. Lautenbach). Zion Lutheran "Red" Church, Orwigsburg, Schuylkill County.

The Catholic equivalent, from Ecclesiasticus 38, verse 23, appears in English on several Catholic stones in the Bally Catholic church graveyard:

> Remember my Judgment for
> thine also shall be so.
> Yesterday for me, today for thee.
> (For example, Charles Rehr, d. 1865, Bally, Berks County)

Of course, the shift from German to English did not happen overnight. In many graveyards one can see the change in family plots where the early stones have a German inscription and the later have an English one.[34] The stones may even have been made from the same design blanks and inscribed by the same carver. C. Laubenbach of Schuylkill Haven, Schuylkill County, for example, was active throughout much of Schuylkill County in the 1860s through the 1890s (Figs. 10 and 12). He carved epitaphs in German using the fraktur style lettering and epitaphs in English with non-German lettering. The change went beyond the language: the German lettering style was abandoned when English was adopted, making the change apparent before one gets close enough to read the stone.

Bilingual stones appeared during the transition from German to English[35] (Fig. 13). Some are pure German-language epitaphs inscribed on blanks which already contained standard English-language texts such as "At Rest," "Father," or "Mother." This form of bilingualism appeared in the 1840s and died out as German became used less and less on the markers. The last stones in this form date from approximately 1900.

Of more interest are stones which include both German and English text within the main epitaph. In the Orwigsburg region of Schuylkill County the majority of these bilingual stones appeared in the 1840s and 1850s. At Muddy Creek in Lancaster these stones first appear in the 1850s and survive into the 1880s. Two forms of these bilingual stones appear. First there is the stone with the biography duplicated in German and English.

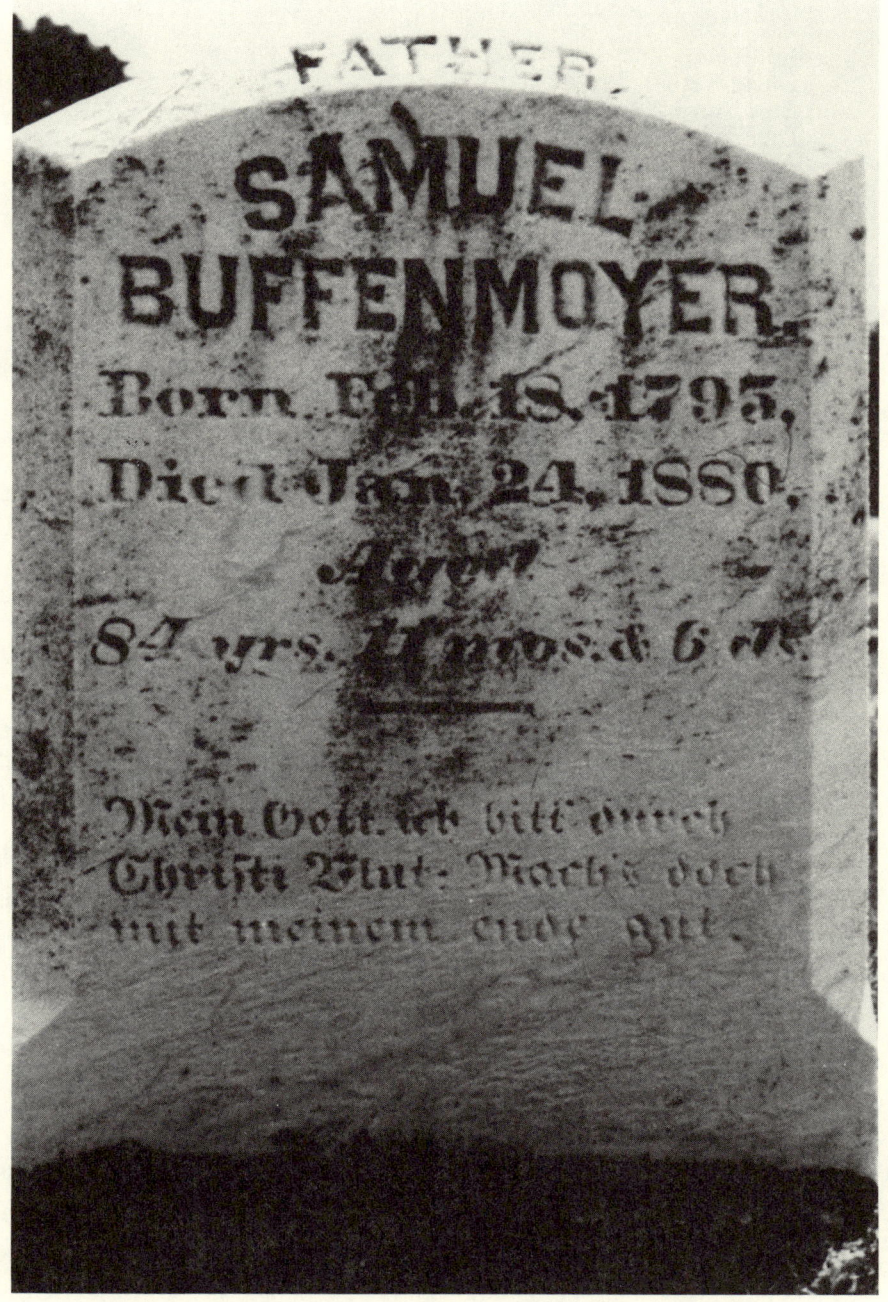

Fig. 13. Samuel Boffenmoyer (d. 1880) received a bilingual stone. Bernville, Berks County.

> In Memory of
> David Ketner
> Born April 29th 1789
> Died July 14th 1859
> Aged 70 Yrs 2 Months
> and 15 Days.
>
> Zum Andenken an
> David Ketner
> Geboren den 29ien April 1789
> Gestorben den 14ien Juli 1859
> Alter 70 Jahre 2 Monate
> und 15 Tage.
>   (Zion Lutheran "Red" Church, Orwigsburg,
>   Schuylkill County)

At the Red Church in Orwigsburg both languages appear on the same face of the stone. At Muddy Creek some of the stones will have the German inscription on one side (obverse or reverse) and the English on the other. Sometimes the second language epitaph is abbreviated, even to the point of duplicating only the name in German script. This form of bilingual epitaph seems to acknowledge the ethnic origin of the dead as well as the fact that not all the dead person's family and friends could still read German. These "Rosetta Stones" highlight the loss of German as a reading language by many of the Pennsylvania Germans during the nineteenth century.[36]

The loss of German started early in parts of the Pennsylvania German region. The Pennsylvania Germans had to deal with their English-speaking neighbors on a continual basis. High German was the language used in the church services. The need to speak English on an almost daily basis had an early effect in some areas. Henry Melchior Muhlenberg, sent to the colonies from Halle, Germany, in 1842, noted the need for English-language sermons in order to keep the people from leaving the church.[37] His son, Henry Muhlenberg, said in 1805 that he would support a new Lutheran seminary only if "young men be educated so as to be able to preach also in English."[38] Many of the immigrants who arrived during the second wave of immigration in the nineteenth century felt strongly that their German culture and language should be maintained. These people helped to revive an interest in German.[39] German was reinforced in other ways as well. One was the large number of German-language newspapers and almanacs.[40]

Another was translating the popular "camp meeting" songs into Pennsylvania German dialect. The dialect versions remained popular through the 1950s and into the 1960s.[41] Although there were congregations which dropped German early, many services continued to be held in German with some German services lasting through the 1930s. The latest use of German on gravestones documented so far is a 1933 stone in Bernville. Another conservative part of the culture was the Pennsylvania German dialect, which is still spoken in parts of the Pennsylvania German region today, with some churches having occasional dialect services.[42] There were strong motivations and forces from both directions: the keeping and the dropping of High German and the dialect as the language of church and home.

The second form of bilingual stone is more complex. On these stones part of the epitaph is in German and part in English. One stone from an unnamed graveyard in Orwigsburg, Schuylkill County, has the German familial biography for Elisabeth Orwig in German, complete with the sermon text. Underneath are two verses in English from a funeral hymn.

Denkmal
für
Elisabeth
Tochter von Wane u. Elisabeth Orwig
geboren am 24 Marz 1816
und Starb den 23 September 1843

Alter 27 Jahre 5 Monate 29 Tage
Text: 2 Thimothy 4 Cap V 78

Memorial
for
Elisabeth
Daughter of Wane and Elisabeth Orwig
Born on the 24th of March, 1816
And died the 23rd of September, 1843

Aged 27 years, 5 months, 29 days.
Text: 2 Timothy, Chapter 4, Verse 78.

Well, she is gone and now in Heaven
She sings his praise who died for her
And to her hand a harp is given
And she is a heavenly worshipper

O let me think of all she said
And all the kindness she gave
And let me do it now shes dead
And sleeping in her lowly grave

Other stones have the biography in English, with the sermon reference, the funeral hymn, or a religious verse in German. These stones are in effect speaking to two cultures, not just to one culture in the process of learning a new language.

For the Pennsylvania German the important thing is to bear witness to the existence of the dead. We learn from a gravestone, for example, that the name of the deceased was Samuel Buffenmoyer; that he was born on February 18, 1795 and died on January 24, 1880; and that he lived to be 84 years, 11 months and 6 days old. His remains rest in peace in the Brickerville Lutheran Church cemetery. The verse on his stone reminds us that we are saved through Christ's sacrifice:

Mein Gott - ich bitt durch Christi Blut: Mache doch mit meinem ende gut.	My God, I pray by means of Christ's blood, Make my end be good.

He was born, he lived, he died, and we knew him. He looked for salvation through the Lord. This is what was important in the eighteenth century and what was still important in the twentieth century.

One can trace the change in artistic fashions related to death as the skull becomes a cherub becomes a willow becomes a flower. On English-language stones, the evolution in artistic motifs is paralleled and reinforced by the verses used in the epitaphs. These verses evolve from *Memento Mori* of the "Reader, stop as you pass by" variety to ones stating that the dead person is resting in Jesus or has gone to his eternal home. A movement takes place from the 1700s through the 1800s away from the physical representation of death (skulls, death's heads, skeletons in art and "Here lies the body of" in the epitaphs) to a metaphorical presence (urns, cut flowers, hands pointing upwards in art and "Asleep in Jesus" in epitaphs). At the same time, there is a movement from showing little concern with the spiritual state of the dead (the death's heads and *Memento Mori* are all very physical) toward the belief and knowledge that the dead one is alive and well in his new heavenly home (gates of heaven and angels taking the dead heavenward in art, ideas of reaching salvation, making the final journey and in reaching a new home in epitaphs).[43] On the German-language stones, the artistic evolution is very clear, but there is no similar evolution in the epitaphs. Beyond the switch from *Hier Ruhet* (Here Rests) to *Denkmal für* (A memorial for), no such textual change paralleling the change in designs exists on the Pennsylvania German stones. The epitaphs continue to be concerned with who the person was. Once the Pennsylvania German gravestones start appearing in English, the attitudes shown among the English-speaking population start to appear in the epitaphs.

This is not to say that an evolution in attitudes toward death did not exist among the German-speaking population. It simply becomes harder to document such changes, if they do exist, using only the gravestones as evidence. Any changes which did occur never predominated over the primary object of reviewing the life of the deceased. It would be interesting to track the texts used for the funeral sermons and the hymns sung at the funeral services to see if they show any pattern of change over time. It could well be that which sermon texts and hymns were used changed over time and that these changes record the evolving attitudes as reflected by the English-language epitaphs.

Popular printed materials tended to have a conservative influence on each language tradition. <u>Der Zånger am Grabe</u>, a German-language book of hymns for the dead first published in 1842, included a list of popular funeral sermon texts.[44] By at least the 1860s, English-language stonecutters were publishing booklets, or catalogs, of epitaphs from which patrons could choose.[45] The more people choosing from such works, the slower would any change in attitudes manifest itself.

One can also trace the use of ethnic markers. Many of the early gravestone decorations stem from inherited motifs of Pennsylvania German folk art. Some of the later ones may represent a conscious attempt to make a statement in the face of the mid-nineteenth century culture clash, a stressful period which can be seen in the bilingual stones. This same stressful period influenced the codification of plain dress among the Amish and Mennonites into a uniform and saw the first appearance of gaily painted hex signs on barns in Berks and Lehigh Counties.[46] The German language became an ethnic marker and the strength of the ethnic tradition in local regions can be measured by how long German was used on the stones.

Finally, the interplay between cultures can be studied, as in the Pennsylvania German adoption of the mainstream, popular art forms. The importance of English to a local region can be estimated by how soon the switch was made from German to English on the stones. The appearance of English surnames, or those of other ethnic groups, on stones in a graveyard hints at settlement and intermarriage patterns.[47]

Now, the author should take his cue from John 16, verse 7, found on a stone in Bernville, Berks County, which says: "It is expedient For you that I go away."

NOTES

An earlier version of this paper was presented at the Annual Meeting of the Association for Gravestone Studies held at Rutgers University in New Brunswick, New Jersey on June 29, 1985. I am grateful for the comments made by Don Yoder and by members of the audience at the original presentation.

1. Russel Wieder Gilbert, *A Picture of the Pennsylvania Germans*, (Gettysburg, PA, The Pennsylvania Historical Association, 1971), p. 3.
2. See Don Yoder, "Religious Patterns of the Dutch Country" in *In the Dutch Country*, (Lancaster, Pennsylvania Dutch Folklore Center, n.d.), pp. 6-8.
3. See, for example, Gilbert, op. cit., pp. 12-14, and Frederick S. Weiser, "Baptismal Certificate and Gravemarker: German Folk Art at the Beginning and the End of Life" in Ian M.G. Quimby and Scott T. Swank, eds., *Perspectives on American Folk Art*, (New York, Norton), p. 134.
4. The gravestones of Pennsylvania have not received the attention which those of New England have. Some of the works include Preston A. Barba, *Pennsylvania German Tombstones: A Study in Folk Art*, (Allentown, PA, Schlechter's, 1954); Thomas E. Graves, "Leibsten Kinder und Werwandten: Death and Ethnicity," *Keystone Folklore*, NS-2:1/2 (1983):6-14; Graves, *The Pennsylvania German Hex Sign: A Study in Folk Process*, unpub. Ph.D. dissertation, (Univ. of PA, 1984), pp. 82, 223-225, 377, 425, 481; Frank E. McDonald, "Pennsylvania German Tombstone Art of Lebanon County, Pennsylvania," *Pennsylvania Folklife*, XXV:1 (Autumn, 1975):2-19; John Joseph Stoudt, *Pennsylvania German Folk Art: An Interpretation*, (Allentown, PA, Schlechter's, 1966); Weiser, op. cit.; and Louis Winkler, "Pennsylvania German Astronomy and Astrology IV: Tombstones," *Pennsylvania Folklife*, XXII:2 (Winter 1972-73):42-45.
5. Some of the earliest gravestones are in the surviving Mennonite graveyards in Germantown. The earliest date found on a stone at Axe's burial ground is 1716. This Germantown graveyard was established for the Mennonite community in 1692. See Joseph S. Miller and Marcus Miller, *An Index and Description of The Mennonites of Southeastern Pennsylvania, 1683-1983*, (Philadelphia, Germantown Mennonite Church Corporation and the Mennonite Historians of Eastern Pennsylvania, n.d.) For consistency, these stones will not be discussed since the focus of this paper is the gravestones of the Lutheran and Reformed groups.
6. The markers used by the Mennonites during the colonial period were comparatively small and unadorned. Decorations that did appear include hearts and trees-of-life. The Victorian stones generally followed the trends outlined in this paper, although not the full range of designs were used. The Mennonite and Amish stones are much plainer because of

these groups' ideas of "plainness," ideas shared by the early Puritans and the Quakers.
7. For the Lutheran congregation, see Frederick S. Weiser, S.T.M., "The Lutherans" in Robert Grant Crist, ed., *Penn's Example to the Nations: 300 Years of the Holy Experiment*, (Harrisburg, Pennsylvania Council of Churches for the Pennsylvania Religious Tercentenary Committee, 1987), pp. 74-75. For the Reformed congregations, see John B. Frantz, Ph.D., "United Church of Christ" in Crist, op. cit., pp. 129-146, and "Historic Churches of WBYO Land" in the 20th Anniversary Issue of *WBYO Wavelength*, (published by radio station WBYO in Boyertown, PA, 1980), vol. 13, p. 27. The latter publication describes and illustrates many of the historical churches of this region of all denominations.
8. Frances Lichten, *Folk Art of Rural Pennsylvania*, (New York, Charles Scribner's, 1946), p. 131.
9. McDonald, op. cit. Cast iron markers are mentioned and illustrated by Henry C. Mercer, *The Bible in Iron*, (Doylestown, PA, The Bucks County Historical Society, 1961), p. 250 and plate 392 and Henry J. Kauffman, *Early American Ironware*, (New York, Weathervane, 1967), pp. 25, 28, but the examples illustrated, with dates of 1747 and 1825, are from New Jersey. Pennsylvania had a large iron industry, so this form of marker may have been produced and used there. Iron markers were also used in the mid-nineteenth century by the Pennsylvania Germans who migrated into Virginia and West Virginia. See Elmer Lewis Smith, John G. Stewart, and M. Ellsworth Kyger, *The Pennsylvania Germans of the Shenandoah Valley*, (Allentown, Schlechter's, 1964), p. 224.
10. McDonald, op. cit., pp. 18-19.
11. Lewis Miller, *Sketches and Chronicles*, (York, PA, The Historical Society of York County, 1966), p. 63. Other early graveyards are illustrated on pp. 12, 28 (a Mennonite burial ground), 109 (Prospect Hill, a garden cemetery).
12. Weiser, op. cit., p. 160. Almost no work identifying individual carvers has been done in Pennsylvania. The names of nineteenth century carvers are often found at the bottom of the stone. These names have not been systematically collected. McDonald made a start by grouping stones by styles. One work which does mention carvers is Smith, Stewart, and Kyger, op. cit., pp. 224-5, 227. This book is concerned with the Pennsylvania Germans who migrated from Pennsylvania to Virginia and West Virginia, and the carvers mentioned are from the Shenandoah Valley and not from the core area of Pennsylvania. This area of research is currently wide open in Pennsylvania.
13. Weiser, op. cit., pp. 134-61.
14. I have seen such baptismal certificates in the fraktur collection of the Historical Society of Berks County. This information is sometimes added in pencil and sometimes on the back of the certificate, making it hard to spot these additions from the illustrations in the published collections.
15. Don Yoder (personal communication) remembers seeing one Berks County stone which listed the hymn sung at the house, the hymn sung at church, and the hymn sung at the graveside.
16. Philippe Aries, *The Hour of our Death*, (New York, Knopf, 1981), pp. 409-556.
17. Barba, op. cit., 140-151; Lichten, op. cit. For other examples of German markers, see Ernst Schlee, *German Folk Art* (Tokyo, New York and San Francisco, 1980), pp. 218-219. For German wrought iron markers, see Karl von Spiess, <u>*Bauernkunst, Ihre Art und ihr Sinn*</u>, (Berlin, Herbert Stubenrauch, 1943), pp. 206-208. See also *"Grabdenkmäler"* and *"Totenbrett"* in Oswald A. Erich and Richard Beitl, <u>*Wörterbuch der deutschen Volkskunde*</u>, 1st ed., (Leipzig, Alfred Kroner, 1936), pp. 256-258, 718.
18. Barba, op. cit., p. 170.
19. Stoudt, op. cit. p. 378-80. He illustrates them again with no comment in *Sunbonnets and Shoofly Pies. A Pennsylvania Dutch Cultural History*, (New York, Castle Books, 1973), p. 160.

20. Lichten, op. cit.
21. These theories have been put forward in conversations with, among other people, Tim Kloberdanz and Don Yoder.
22. Schlee, op. cit. Painted wooden markers are illustrated in Klaus Beitl, *Volksglaube. Zeugnisse Religiser Volkunst*, (Salzburg and Vienna, Residenz Verlag, 1978), figures 46 a-d (notes on pp. 156-158).
23. Stoudt, *Pennsylvania German Folk Art*, op cit. Stoudt's whole hypothesis is that all of Pennsylvania German art is a manifestation of religious beliefs. This theme runs through Stoudt's entire book, but readers can consult chapter 4: "Symbol, Image, and Literary Expression" (pp. 99-118) for brief descriptions of various motifs. His works are very detailed and well documented. The main argument that has arisen is the question of whether colonial artists or their clientele knew these religious connections.
24. Winkler, op. cit.
25. Barba, op. cit., pp. 11-12.
26. Barba, ibid, pp. 9-10. See also Graves, *The Pennsylvania Hex Sign*, op. cit., pp. 444-448.
27. Barba, op. cit.; Graves, *The Pennsylvania Hex Sign*, op. cit.; and "Leibsten Kinder", op. cit. Hex signs on barns are found only among members of the church groups of the Pennsylvania Germans. The Amish and Mennonites do not have hex signs.
28. Allan I. Ludwig, *Graven Images: New England Stonecarving and its Symbols, 1650-1815*, (Middletown, CT, Wesleyan Univ. Press, 1966), pp. 225-232.
29. C. Schuchhardt, *Schliemann's Discoveries of the Ancient World*, (New York, Avenel Books, 1979), pp. 177-205. The rosette and other related geometric designs have been traced back to Sumaria, where these designs were used to decorate pottery.
30. Graves, *The Pennsylvania German Hex Sign*, op. cit., pp. 422-430.
31. Graves, ibid, pp. 223-225, and "Leibsten Kinder", op. cit.
32. For examples of Victorian motifs on the gravestones of the English-speaking population of the United States, see Edmund V. Gillon, Jr., *Victorian Cemetery Art*, (New York, Dover, 1972).
33. For an example, see the Currier and Ives print, "The Mother's Dream," with the angel carrying the dead baby's soul heavenward, reproduced in Martha K. Pike and Janice Gray Armstrong, *A Time to Mourn. Expressions of Grief in Nineteenth Century America*, (New York, The Museums at Stony Brook, 1980), p. 143. *Das Herz des Menschen, ein Temple Gottes, oder eine Werkstätte des Satans*, (Reading, PA, Heinrich B. Sage, 1822), fig. 10, and its English translation, *The Heart of Man, A Temple of God or the Habitation of Satan*, (Harrisburg, Theo F. Scheffer, n.d.) shows an angel at the deathbed of a "saintly man" and another one carrying a Bible as it flies through the air. The small soul effigy is being taken heavenward via God's words which extend from God's mouth to the effigy. Figure 8 in these books shows the death of the ungodly man who is cast into eternal fire by God. In Figure 10 the angel is pointing upwards; in Figure 8 she is pointing downwards. In Figure 8 the devils and demons await the soul, which has apparently not yet left the body. See also the numerous prints of angels carrying George Washington heavenward which were popular in the first couple of decades of the nineteenth century. Two examples are reproduced in Anita Schorsch, *Mourning Becomes America. Mourning Art in the New Nation*, (Harrisburg, Pennsylvania Historical and Museum Commission, 1976), plates 19/50, 20/51.
34. Graves, "Leibsten Kinder", op. cit., pp. 9-11.
35. Ibid.
36. Bilingual stones are not unique to the Pennsylvania Germans. Halporn, for example, illustrates two stones with a mixture of Hebrew and English texts and one with a Hebrew and German text. Roberta Halporn, *Lessons from the Dead*, (Brooklyn, Highly Specialized Promotions, 1979), pp. 12, 22, 24. As a side note, the German Jews were an important part

of the second wave of immigration from Germany to the United States from 1840 to 1880.
37. Weiser, "The Lutherans," op. cit., p. 75; and Doerries, op. cit., p.77.
38. Doerries, ibid.
39. Ibid., pp. 77-79.
40. See, for example, Louis Winkler, "Pennsylvania German Astronomy and Astrology XVI: German Language Almanacs," *Pennsylvania Folklife*, 28:2 (Winter, 1978/79), pp. 18-25.
41. Yoder, "Religious Patterns," op. cit.; and *Pennsylvania Spiritual*, (Lancaster, Pennsylvania Folklife Society, 1961).
42. I have tapes of story-telling sessions held almost entirely in the dialect from as recently as the Spring of 1987. Concerning the dialect, see, for example, Richard Druckenbrod, *Mir Lanne Deitsch*, (Allentown, by the author, 1981); William T. Parsons, "Pennsylfawnisch Deitsch und Pfalzer: Dialect Comparisons Old and New", *Pennsylvania Folklife*, 31:3 (Spring, 1982), pp. 117-127; and Claude K. Deischer, "My Experience with the Dialect," *Pennsylvania Folklife*, 23:4 (Summer, 1974), pp. 47-48. Concerning dialect services, see Don Yoder, "The Dialect Church Service in the Pennsylvania German Culture," *Pennsylvania Folklife*, 27:4 (Summer, 1978), pp. 2-13.
43. Graves, "Changes in Attitudes Toward Death as Reflected in the Gravestones of St. David's Episcopal Church (Radnor, PA)", unpub. M.A. paper, Univ. of PA, 1979.
44. Carl G. Herman, *Der Zänger am Grabe* (Kutztown, PA, 1842). This book has gone through many reprints.
45. *A Collection of Epitaphs suitable for Monumental Inscriptions from various Sources*, (Harrisburg, John Beatty, Stone-Cutter, 1867). Earlier catalogs of epitaphs may exist.
46. Don Yoder, "Sectarian Costume Research in the United States", in *Forms Upon the Frontier*, (Logan, Utah, Utah State Univ., 1969), pp. 41-75; and Graves, *The Pennsylvania German Hex Sign*, op. cit., pp. 80-83.
47. Of course, all of the other possible ways to learn from graveyards as outlined by Halporn (op. cit.) are also available to those studying Pennsylvania German gravestones.

1. One of Pennsylvania's many eighteenth-century rural graveyards. Lower Marsh Creek Presbyterian Cemetery, Fairfield, Adams County.

EARLY PENNSYLVANIA GRAVEMARKERS

Photographs and text by
Daniel and Jessie Lie Farber

The photographs on the following pages are an introduction to the variety and charm of Pennsylvania's early gravestone art. This group of photographs is presented as a companion piece to the preceding article by Thomas Graves. We made the photographs in the spring of 1984.

In June, 1988 The Association for Gravestone Studies will hold its annual conference in Lancaster, Pennsylvania, a short drive from several graveyards rich in fine examples of early carving. We hope that Thomas Graves's article, our photographs and the 1988 conference will stimulate interest and encourage further research in Pennsylvania gravestone art.

2. One of several handsome bird carvings in the Fairfield graveyard. Samuel Reynold, 1758; slate, 18" high.

3. An unusual winged beast carved on a damaged marker in Amish farm country. John Midlto, 1739, Chestnut Level, Lancaster County; slate, 20" high.

4. The two animals on this stone appear to be the carver's primitive attempt to depict the rooster, a symbol of fertility. Rudolph Oberle, 1777, Hellertown, Northampton County; sandstone, 31" high.

5. Hearts and flowers are used in a variety of ways, here in combination to depict a tree of life. This lightly incised carving is on a stone inscribed in German. Elisabet Kunsin, 1794, Littlestown, Adams County; sandstone, 27" high.

6. This tree of life, cut in high relief, decorates a marker that has no inscription. Bergstrasse Lutheran Churchyard, Ephrata, Lancaster County; sandstone, 40" high.

CHERUBS

7. Chubby figures carrying Bibles or branches of fruit are found in the area around Bernville. The stones are inscribed in beautiful, but deteriorated, German fraktur lettering. Name illegible, 1775, Christ Little Tupelhocken Churchyard, Bernville, Berks County; sandstone, 38" high.

8. A little face and circles decorate a stone with "M 1811 D" its only inscription. M.D., 1811, Muddy Creek Lutheran Church Cemetery, Ephrata, Lancaster County; sandstone, 30" high.

AND WINGED FACES ...

9. This winged face adorned with hearts and halo is one of many fanciful effigies carved on gray stone in and around Brickerville. The markers have been set in concrete. Anna Millerin, 1825, Emmanuel Lutheran Churchyard, Brickerville, Lancaster County; possibly sandstone, 36" high.

10. A unique effigy in a yard containing other one-of-a-kind designs cut by the same unidentified carver. Thomas Millroie, 1747, Chestnut Level, Lancaster County; slate, 19" high.

11. Hearts sometimes replace the traditional skull over crossbones, as on this tympanum carving. Name illegible, 1757, New Goshenhoppen Churchyard, East Greenville, Montgomery County; sandstone, 27" high.

12. Skull and crossbones in high relief at base of stone. Johan Bngl(?), circa 1785, United Church of Christ Churchyard, Blainsport, Lancaster County; sandstone, 45" high.

AND CELESTIAL BODIES ...

13. The waning moon and other heavenly bodies are design motifs common to stones in Muddy Creek and Bergstrasse Lutheran Church Cemeteries. Their unidentified carver usually cut only a partial inscription or no inscription. No inscription, circa 1800, Muddy Creek Lutheran Churchyard, Ephrata, Lancaster County; sandstone.

14. Floral decorations and rosettes are widely used, the hourglass rarely. Leonhard Miller, 1794, Emanuel Lutheran Churchyard, Brickerville, Lancaster County; sandstone, 39" high.

15a.

AND A FEW "PORTRAITS."

15b.

15 a,b. Wingless faces are rare. 15a. No inscription, circa 1800, Muddy Creek Lutheran Churchyard, Ephrata, Lancaster County; sandstone, 40" high. 15b. Salome Eichelberger, 1793, Hanover, York County; slate, 21" high.

CARVING STYLES RANGE FROM PRIMITIVE TO SOPHISTICATED.

16. Primitive marker, possibly a footstone. KD, 1767, New Goshenhoppen Churchyard, East Greenville, Montgomery County; sandstone, 12" high.

17. Skillfully executed life and death symbols. John Clark, 1776, Chestnut Level, Lancaster County; slate, 34" high.

DEATH MOTIFS ARE USED INFREQUENTLY.

18. Mortality symbols: skull flanked by hourglass and candle in holder with flickering flame (?). George Junt, 1770, Bergstrasse Lutheran Churchyard, Ephrata, Lancaster County; sandstone, 36" high.

19a. The outer circle of this inscription reads, "KOM STERBLICHER BETRACHTE MICH" (Come, mortal one, consider me). The inner circle reads, "WAS ICH B," probably the beginning of, "Was Ich bin, so wirst auch dirch" (What I am, so you will also be).

ARE IN GERMAN...

19b. The reverse of the marker in photograph 19a. Catrina Cromirin, 1783, Penryn, Lancaster County; sandstone, 21" high.

20. Early stone inscribed in English. This striking marker uses the head and wings of the effigy to form the traditional eighteenth-century tympanum-and-shoulder gravestone configuration. Elisabeth Steel, 1749, Chestnut Level, Lancaster County; sandstone, 21" high.

ARE IN ENGLISH.

21. This stone stands in a yard dominated by German inscriptions. Elizabeth Weidman, circa 1800, Emanuel Lutheran Churchyard, Brickerville, Lancaster County; a gray stone, probably sandstone, set in concrete; 23" high.

SOME MARKERS ARE ONLY PARTIALLY INSCRIBED ...

22. Partially inscribed stone with a blank area where one expects to find further data, a curiosity seen on a number of stones in the area by the same area carver. Freyen is the feminine form of Frey. H. Freyen, Muddy Creek Lutheran Churchyard, Ephrata, Lancaster County; sandstone.

23. Stone with no inscription, circa 1800. Muddy Creek Lutheran Churchyard, Ephrata, Lancaster County; sandstone, 31" high.

24. Interesting symbolism on one of the uninscribed stones that appear to be the work of the same Lancaster County carver. Is the sun rising or setting over water, or is it peeking through clouds? Circa 1800, Bergstrasse Lutheran Churchyard, Ephrata, Lancaster County; sandstone, 39" high.

A LARGE PERCENTAGE OF THE STONES

25 a,b. Typical uninscribed marker with decorative carving on both sides. Circa 1800, Muddy Creek Lutheran Churchyard, Ephrata, Lancaster County; sandstone, 26" high.

ARE CARVED ON BOTH FACES.

26 a,b. Typical example of a marker decorated on one side, inscribed on the reverse. The tree of life is similar to others that appear to be by the same area carver. Rudolf Oberly, 1780, Christ Union Church, Lower Saucon Township, near Hellertown, Northampton County; sandstone, 29" high on decorated (excavated) side.

NINETEENTH-CENTURY MARKERS ARE DECORATED WITH

27a.

27b.

27 a,b,c,d. Four examples of traditional nineteenth-century symbols, three with handsome fraktur lettering. Huffs Churchyard, Huffs Church, Berks County; marble. 27a. Friedrich Sigmund, 1860; 58" high. 27b. Philip Blumbauer, 1851, 47" high.

FINE EXAMPLES OF TRADITIONAL SYMBOLISM OF THAT PERIOD.

27c.

27d.

27c. James Cunningham, 1868, 41" high.   27d. James R. Menich, 1862, 30" high.

28a.

28b.

IS UNIQUE IN ITS DIVERSITY AND CHARM.

28c.

28 a,b,c. Three unique examples of Pennsylvania's finest gravestone art. **28a.** Name illegible, 1750, Christ Lutheran Church, Stouchsburg, Berks County; sandstone, 33" high. **28b.** No inscription, circa 1800, Muddy Creek Lutheran Churchyard, Ephrata, Lancaster County; sandstone, 40" high. (For reverse of this stone see 14b.) **28c.** Jane Waugh, 1770, Lower Marsh Creek Presbyterian Cemetery, Fairfield, Adams County; slate, 30" high.

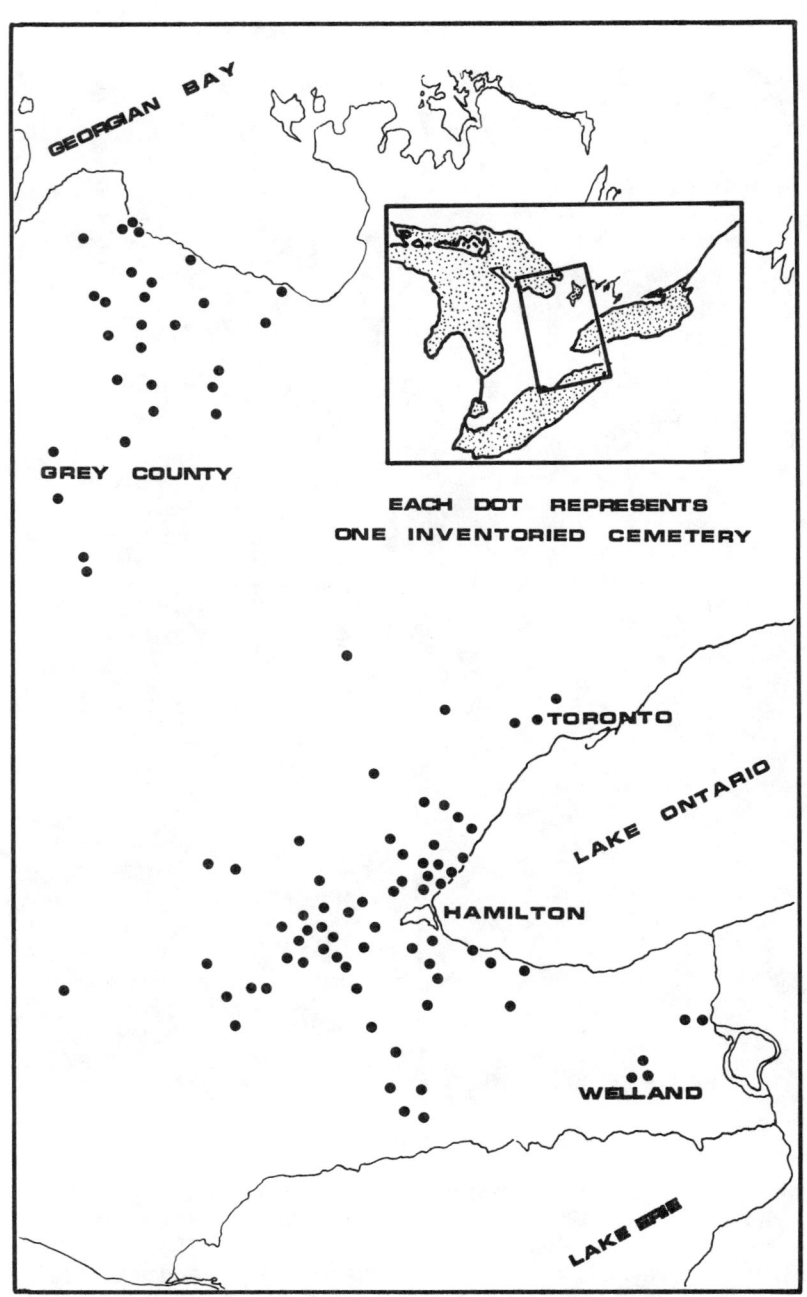

Map of Ontario

ONTARIO GRAVESTONES

Darrell A. Norris

Introduction

Few facets of nineteenth-century material culture are as evocative as the gravestone. No other historical artifact matches the gravestone's many advantages as a cultural indicator. Its merits include widespread distribution, visibility, durability, relative immobility, and sheer numbers. As an important bonus, the age of gravestones is reasonably easy to establish. To these advantages may be added the gravestone's summary profile of individual lives, its reflection of contemporary taste and symbolic expression, and, sometimes, its attribution to a particular carver or manufacturer. Moreover, the gravestone rarely stands in splendid isolation. Its groupings, from small family plots to urban necropolises, are rich lodes of spatial meaning. Geographers have considered ways in which communities of the dead were planned, sited, named, subdivided, and filled to echo the ideals and norms of society (Kniffen, 1967; Francaviglia, 1971; Jeane, 1978; Darden, 1972; Zelinsky, 1975). Few cultural landscape features offer greater scope for the geographer concerned with North America's past. Despite its morbid and awkward name, necrogeography has been a lively branch of cultural geography.

Yet, even allowing for the excellent work on gravestones and cemeteries produced by cultural geographers, folk historians, and archaeologists, the shades of meaning conveyed by the gravestone remain in some respects unexplored. This deficiency of detailed observation and inference is most evident in the case of gravestone design, particularly for the period of exuberant design and burgeoning popular culture between the late eighteenth and early twentieth century. One reason for the limited work on this topic is that gravestones of the early industrial era pose an immense taxonomic problem. How does one cope with a repertoire of design expression which embraced apparently endless variants of form, size, decorative treatment, verbal inscription, and material composition? The immense iconographic potential of this repertoire needs no emphasis. The variety is immediately evident in most Victorian cemeteries, and conspicuously absent in the modern rule-bound memorial garden.

The ordinary Victorian commemoration of death was anything but egalitarian; it was remarkably expressive and varied (Pike and Armstrong, 1980). And, as much as it celebrated the dead, nineteenth-century burial accommodated the dispositions of the living. To comprehend the gravestone as both a commercially sold object *and* as a vehicle of Victorian expression requires a systematic, flexible, and subtle approach to classification and contextual analysis. Applying such a classification with reasonable confidence in the results obtained requires numerous examples of gravestone design through time and across space. Most importantly, we need to blend our understanding of gravestones with information about the people who commissioned them, those who made and sold them (Wallace, 1985), and those who died to deserve them.

This essay addresses these themes using evidence drawn from the Province of Ontario, Canada. Aggregate results are presented based on a widespread inventory of cemeteries in rural southern Ontario undertaken between 1975 and 1979 by McMaster University geography students under my direction. The inventory included over five thousand gravestones erected between 1800 and 1909. A total of 105 rural cemeteries were inventoried. I have selected a number of case studies which illustrate ways in which gravestone evidence can be integrated with broader aspects of nineteenth-century society, especially its social and cultural geography.

Previous work focused on Ontario cemeteries and gravestones includes a small volume of photographs by Carole Hanks (1974), an assessment of gravestones as a demographic source (Osborne, 1974), recent work devoted to cemetery design and regulation (Hall and Bowden, 1986), and a specialized treatment of the carving of human or divine figures as decorative motifs (Stone and Russell, 1986). An Ontario Genealogical Society monograph (Knight, 1973) features some case studies, and Nancy-Lou Patterson (1976) presents a fascinating discussion of the tree-of-life form as an instance of persistent folk tradition among German-Canadian settlers. As far as I am aware, however, the literature contains no overview of memorial practice in Ontario, its ties to New England folk tradition, or its parallels with nineteenth-century developments in the United States.

Ontario

The geographer Peirce Lewis has characterized the Niagara border region as one of the sharpest cultural divides in North America. His topic was another *sine qua non* of material-cultural study, the vernacular house. Ontario began as Upper Canada, a by-product of the American Revolution and of the diaspora of Loyalists (Tories) from a lost cause to remote settlement nuclei at both ends of Lake Ontario, in a land wrested from France in the eighteenth century's other decisive North American conflict. Scrutiny of Ontario's earliest colonists under English rule reveals a heterogeneous cultural profile; those of Dutch background and other New Yorkers were relatively numerous, as were discharged troops from England's polyglot colonial army. Before 1812 land-hungry American emigrants leavened the new society, as did the first arrival of relatively indigent Scots and Irish. Cultural pluralism and exposure to external influences have always characterized Ontario. The War of 1812-14 certainly solidified the province's resolve *not* to slavishly imitate American culture; Ontario's Classical Revival, for example, was muted and rarely ostentatious.

But Ontario's frontier experience, commercial development, and external contacts made for growing similarities with United States social and economic structure, especially that of the lower Great Lakes states. Moreover, the rapid growth of population sustained by immigration between the mid 1820s and early 1850s created a society dominated by Scots and Irish settlers, mainly Protestants, infused with an ethic of toil and progress strikingly similar to that of midwestern American farmers. By the time of Canadian Confederation in 1867, Ontario's people combined a keen national and British Imperial vision with a pragmatic, sometimes even enthusiastic, acceptance of American practice and innovation. It is important to grasp this paradox when one examines just about any aspect of Victorian and Edwardian Ontario society, including memorialization of the dead.

Between 1880 and the First World War, Ontario became increasingly urbanized and industrialized, and absorbed significant numbers of European immigrants in its major manufacturing centers, notably Hamilton and

Toronto. As elsewhere in North America, the material ostentation and security of the Gilded Age veiled growing insecurities and dislocation, including the migration of many rural Ontarians to Western Canada and the United States, the pains of structural or cyclic economic hardship, and the growing dependency of rural areas on external sources (including flows of capital, insurance, credit, produce, consumer goods, information, and people.) Thus rural Ontario's coming of age had actually undermined its sense of autonomy and cultural identity. Its gravestones are a revealing mirror of the province's identity in the wider and changing context of nineteenth-century North American material culture.

Five Roles of the Gravestone

Gravestones are obviously a medium of expression, of communication, but in Ontario as elsewhere this expression is multifaceted. First, the most obvious intent of the gravestone is to provide a fitting and durable memorial to the *individual*. But this role was almost always associated with a second purpose, which was to express the presence and position of the *family* within its immediate community. At the same time, however, gravestones proclaimed and celebrated the fact of *belonging*. Through the collectivity of the cemetery, gravestones replicated ties based on church membership, ethnic background, social standing, and of course place of residence. This third role of the gravestone was to petrify and endorse the complex social order of North American localities.

The fourth role of the gravestone transcended local circumstance. Like Victorian domestic architecture, gravestones reflected shifting currents of *popular taste* in North American society. In Portland, Oregon, no less than in Portland, Maine, death was a catalyst for a vogue or for conformist expression through memorial art. In its fifth role, however, the nineteenth-century gravestone signaled the beginning of mass material culture in the industrial age. As an object of mainly popular, not folk, culture, the gravestone involved makers, sellers, and buyers. In fact it exhibited a close parallel to Victorian furnishings, fittings, and fixtures, for these too disguised standardized forms with a superficial veneer of variety and individuality. It is essential to keep in mind this inherently *commercial* role of the gravestone as one of the first durable consumer goods which combined the illusion of uniqueness with the realities of standardized manufacture.

It is easy to overlook these roles in present-day North America, for the iconography of the gravestone has been impoverished by the fear and cost of death and by the regulation of memorial art. For most of us, eternity will be an undistinguished, compact, high density, even high-rise place of rest. Occupancy costs, the monumental expense of monuments, and the recession of family and community bonds have all stifled a repose which once offered more space, substance, and scope for expression. Thus nineteenth-century gravestone iconography is equally distant from both its craft (and primarily folk-cultural) roots and the muted message it characteristically conveys in twentieth-century mass culture.

Gravestone Form

For cultural geographers, the seminal work on gravestones as cultural expression is the exploratory statement by Richard Francaviglia (1971). Francaviglia's classification of nineteenth and twentieth century American gravestones was based solely on their form. He identified only nine types of monument, two of which were almost exclusively twentieth-century forms. This and other disquieting features of Francaviglia's work were criticized by Jeane (1972) in geography's leading scholarly journal. Nonetheless, Francaviglia's work remains widely read and, I think, is commonly assumed to reflect the realities of gravestone design. For example, Hannon (1973) used a slightly modified version of Francaviglia's classification in a survey of several thousand Pennsylvania gravestones.

Even the most casual observer of Victorian cemeteries immediately sees that obelisks, crosses, and elaborately sculpted forms were greatly outnumbered by vertical slabs. The form of these slabs was mostly determined by the design of their top. Francaviglia identified only two such forms: the Gothic pointed arch, and the round-headed tablet reminiscent of the Mosaic commandments. In fact, however, vertical slabs took many forms, from the plain rectangular gravestone to tops with very complex bilateral symmetry. When Victor Konrad (now Director of Canadian Studies at the University of Maine, Orono) and I designed a standard inventory form for rural Ontario cemeteries, we began with a reconnaissance of several graveyards, noting what appeared to be common vertical slab and other monument forms. The resultant inventory form is illustrated in Figure 1. The more than five thousand gravestones inventoried by our students were all categorized using this standard form. In addition to the nine vertical slab variants illustrated, the form provides for sketches of more detailed treatment of the top and (as we soon discovered) sides of vertical slabs. Computer encoding, recoding, and analysis revealed seven common vertical slab forms in Ontario between 1800 and 1909 (Table 1).

A.G.S. members will be surprised to note that we did not provide for the common New England "bedboard" design in our standard inventory form. As the field surveys progressed after 1975, this deficiency became evident, and fieldworkers were instructed to carefully sketch this tripartite slab and its derivative designs. These are identified as New England forms in Table 1, although of course I recognize that such forms were characteristic of the entire eighteenth-century eastern seaboard and of contemporary England as well. The form does present us with a sense of the weight and persistence of Loyalist cultural baggage in nineteenth-century Ontario. The bedboard stone was, it seems, never dominant after 1800, accounting for no more than 15 percent of the gravestones inventoried in any period of the nineteenth and early twentieth century (Table 1). Nonetheless, this rather faint colonial legacy did prove to be remarkably resilient to Victorian faddishness in memorial design, a feature shared by the Palladian style, also carried forward from eighteenth-century practice (Table 1, and Figure 1, form a) 05).

Baroque complexity of the tops and sides of the vertical slabs in Ontario was especially characteristic of the 1830s, no doubt reflecting the renewal of British immigration and the growing sophistication of the province's early marble works (Table 1). The plain rectangular slab neatly divides the first and second half of the nineteenth century, distinguishing the restricted means of pioneer settlement from the enlarged scope and ostentation of High Victorian rural Ontario.

The segmental arch (Type a) 07), Gothic (Type 2) 09) and Tablet (Type a) 08) vertical slab forms are all illustrated in Figure 1, and exhibit a

FIGURE 1
Inventory Form, Ontario Cemetery Surveys, 1975-1979

Cemetery No. .... Marker No. .... Year of interment ....

FORM (Circle one code no.)
a) *Vertical Slab Variants*
   (Note: Toppled Stones Included)

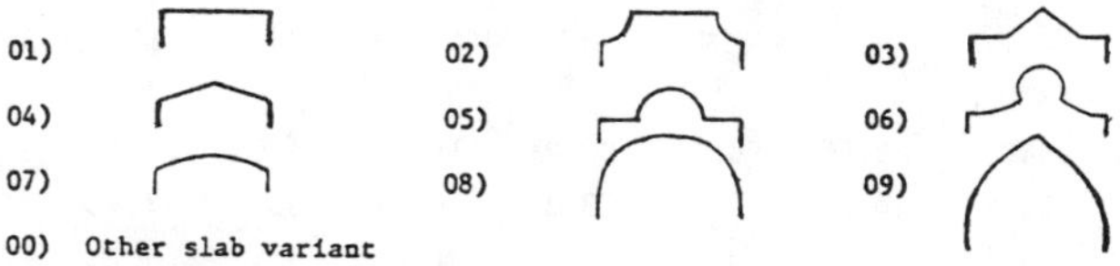

GRID CELL ..../..........

01)   02)   03)
04)   05)   06)
07)   08)   09)

00) Other slab variant
    Please sketch

b) *Near Ground Types*
                    pulpit   scroll
   10)   raised top inscription   lawn
              11)   12)   13)

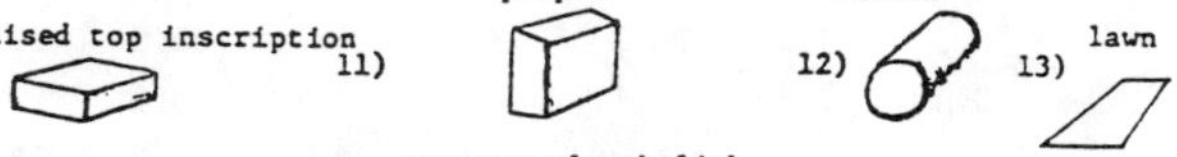

c) *Obelisks*
         simple obelisk   cross-vault obelisk
   14)   15)   16)   other
                                                   (orna-
                                                   mented)
                                                   obelisks

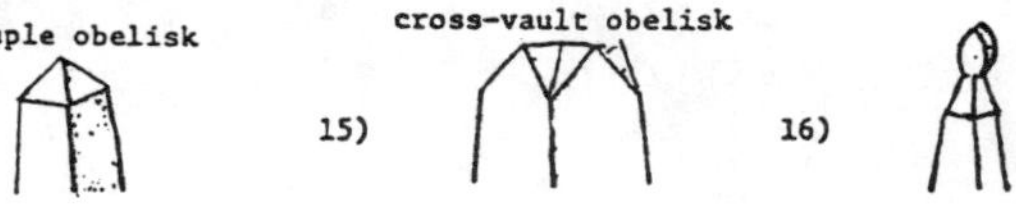

d) *Crosses*   capped by.............
   17)   18)   19)

e) *Other, please sketch*
   20)

f) Granite Block 21)

Lettering is   1) raised   2) incised   3) both

Marker is of   0) D.K.   1) limestone   2) granite   3) slate   4) sandstone   5) other.....

Marker orientation   0) N.A.   1) North   2) East   3) South   4) West

Marker height is   0) less than one,   1)   2)   3)   4)   5)   6)   7)   8)   9)+ feet

Motif is   0) absent   1)   2)   3)   4)
                        willow   urn   clasp   pointer

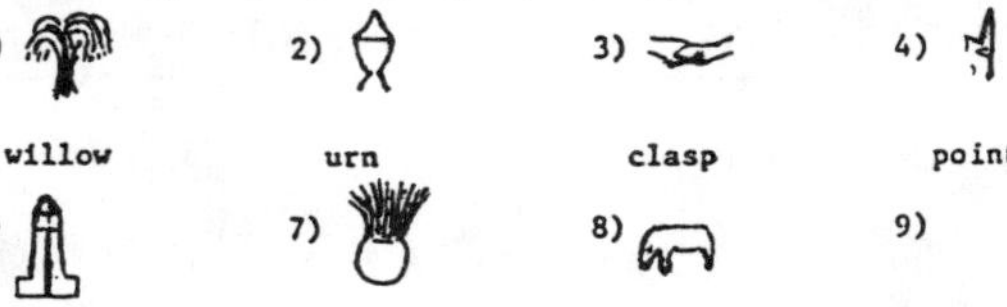

   5)   6)   7)   8)   9)
   bible   obelisk   thistle   lamb   Other: sketch
                                           &/or describ

NOTE: Sculpted motif capping marker (e.g. urn and obelisk) should NOT be recorded.

Marker was supplied by .... (name)
            of .... (place)

Rel'p   First Name   Second Name   Month   Day   Year   Age   Place of Birth, Country
(h,w,s,d,)
....
....
....
....

NOTE: Enter asterisk if illegible, leave blank if absent.

TABLE 1. GRAVESTONE FORMS, RURAL ONTARIO, 1800-1909

FORM	PERIOD								
	1800-1829	1830-1839	1840-1849	1850-1859	1860-1869	1870-1879	1880-1889	1890-1899	1900-1909
	(PERCENT OF GRAVESTONES ERECTED DURING PERIOD)								
VERTICAL SLABS	93.8	89.5	90.4	88.2	84.4	74.5	62.4	43.6	45.2
New England Forms	12.8	14.3	9.8	8.8	11.1	6.0	7.1	6.5	5.7
Palladian	10.4	5.6	3.5	3.8	4.3	6.4	4.2	2.8	1.3
Baroque	3.7	10.6	1.6	0.6	0.8	2.4	1.6	0.3	0.9
Rectangular	41.5	44.1	57.9	48.1	13.0	6.9	3.9	6.5	7.5
Segmental Arch	7.3	1.2	5.7	9.7	26.7	10.0	11.0	9.4*	13.1*
Gothic	3.0	3.7	5.4	7.5	7.8	8.8	5.5	3.0	4.4
Tablet	7.3	2.5	1.6	4.5	14.8	26.2	22.3	9.4	4.1
Other slabs	7.8	7.5	4.9	5.2	5.9	7.8	6.8	5.7*	8.2*
OBELISKS	1.8	3.8	4.1	5.5	8.4	15.3	27.2	35.1	24.4
Simple	0.0	1.9	2.2	2.2	2.6	4.8	7.6	6.1	4.6
Ornamented	1.8	1.9	1.4	2.5	4.4	8.4	14.6	15.3	8.5
Cross-Vault	0.0	0.0	0.5	0.8	1.4	2.1	5.0	13.7	11.3
NEAR-GROUND	3.6	5.5	3.8	4.7	4.7	6.1	4.8	11.5	18.0
Pulpit	0.6	1.2	0.0	0.2	1.2	1.3	2.7	8.9	13.4
Scroll	0.0	0.0	0.0	0.0	0.0	0.0	0.1	0.3	1.2
Raised-top	1.2	4.3	1.6	2.1	1.3	0.4	0.4	0.7	2.1
Lawn	1.8	0.0	2.2	2.4	2.2	4.4	1.6	1.6	1.3
CROSSES	0.0	0.6	0.3	0.5	0.8	1.4	1.6	2.2	3.4
OTHER FORMS	0.8	0.6	1.4	1.1	1.7	2.7	4.0	7.8*	9.0*
TOTAL NO. INVENTORIED	164	161	368	628	775	778	837	672	681

NOTE: Values marked with an asterisk include granite blocks not categorized as such in the original inventory chronological succession of peak popularity between 1860 and 1880 (Table 1). In other words, relatively short-lived *fashion* was not generally typical of Ontario gravestone forms until well into the second half of the nineteenth century. It would be instructive to compare this seemingly late dominance of popular cultural trends with prevailing practice in upstate New York, especially during the second quarter of the nineteenth century.

Obelisks in rural Ontario cemeteries suggest a chronological pattern similar to the three voguish vertical slab forms discussed above--evidence of early *introduction* but very late widespread *acceptance*, confined principally to the 1880s and 1890s (Table 1). Of near-ground marker types, only the pulpit marker was widely manufactured and adopted before 1910 in Southern Ontario (Table 1). Early granite blocks are not specifically reported in Table 1. Granite markers as a whole comprised 44 percent of all inventoried gravestones in the 1890s, and 54 percent during the first decade of this century. Overall, the form of rural Ontario gravestones in the nineteenth century combines modest persistence of traditional designs until the 1860s, with characteristic simplicity of form tempered by early but slow acceptance of key popular styles. From the 1860s on, variety and changing fashion held sway. The shift to modest near-ground memorials was notably slow, presumably stalled by widespread acceptance of early sand-blasted granite blocks and the advent of small (and usually granite) cross-vault obelisks deemed suitable for family burials.

Motifs

Gravestones can be distinguished not only by their form, but also by the presence of decorative or symbolic sculpted motifs. The significance of these motifs is best known through the work of New England scholars (Dethlefsen and Deetz, 1966; Tashjian and Tashjian, 1974; Benes, 1977). Moreover, many contributors to *Markers* and other publications have reported the value of motifs as a key clue to colonial carver identification. My concern is less with the motif as the signature of a carver or evidence of a local practice than with its value as a reflection of widespread popular taste and attitudes. The reader is doubtless familiar with the classically inspired urns, pedestals, and willows which celebrated American death on newly republican soil--so strikingly different from New England's colonial gallery of death's heads, spirits, and angels.

Evidence of motif preference in the Ontario survey is fragmentary for the period prior to 1840 (Table 2). Mourning willows and funerary urns certainly dominated decorative expression, but it is surprising to discover that *all* the most popular motifs in nineteenth-century Ontario are occasionally encountered among the earliest gravestones erected (Table 2). I suspect that the dates on several stones may have been incorrectly read by fieldworkers because of obliteration from weathering.

Through the 1840s and 1850s the willow and urn continued to constitute the majority of all motifs inscribed (Table 2). As with gravestone form, the 1860s were a transitional decade between simplicity and exuberance of expression. The Hand of God in perpetual admonition appeared in appreciable numbers on Ontario gravestones in the 1840s, and remained popular for five decades (Table 2). The Bible motif was a common adjunct of the pulpit marker. The cross was often employed on simple polished granite blocks, and very commonly used in Ontario's Catholic cemeteries. All other motifs reported in Table 2 reflect a prevailing sentimental, romantic, and increasingly secular image of death which characterized the period 1860-1909. The gentle and, one suspects, intentionally ambiguous hand-clasp is a case in point (Figure 1a). Note its remarkable surge in popularity in the 1870s and 1880s (Table 2).

The close of the nineteenth century saw fewer Ontario gravestones decorated with motifs, owing to their comparatively low incidence on obelisks. The turn of the century was also marked by increasing incidence of customized or floral motifs rather than standard symbols evocative of death, faith, or mourning (Table 2). The low but relatively constant use of the thistle is of course simply explained by the Scots presence in Ontario.

I think it is especially noteworthy that in the 1860s and 1870s at least two thirds of *all* rural Ontario gravestones were embellished with motifs. It would be instructive to compare this pattern with, say, rural Michigan or New York. My impression of the latter state has been that nineteenth-century rural New Yorkers were more ready to accept novel *forms* than they were decorative Victorian *embellishment*. The French historian Aries

TABLE 2. MOTIF INCIDENCE, RURAL ONTARIO, 1800-1909

MOTIF	PERIOD								
	1800-1829	1830-1839	1840-1849	1850-1859	1860-1869	1870-1879	1880-1889	1890-1899	1900-1909
	(PERCENT OF RECORDED MOTIFS DURING PERIOD)								
Willow	46.8	55.9	47.4	44.1	23.9	7.3	5.7	2.0	1.6
Urn	12.7	18.6	10.3	7.4	6.6	2.1	2.0	2.9	1.3
Hand of admonition	5.1	1.7	6.4	6.5	9.8	8.4	8.8	3.8	1.0
Rose	2.5	5.1	7.1	11.0	10.9	8.0	12.0	5.8	4.3
Lamb	2.5	1.7	1.3	2.2	7.3	9.1	4.8	2.6	3.3
Clasped hands	3.8	3.4	1.9	1.7	5.7	14.3	18.8	7.3	3.9
Dove	1.3	1.7	0.0	1.2	4.0	5.2	2.4	4.1	1.6
Wreath	2.5	0.0	0.6	1.9	2.9	5.1	6.6	3.8	2.6
Bible	6.3	1.7	2.6	2.9	4.5	7.0	10.9	10.5	9.5
Leaves	5.1	0.0	2.6	2.2	2.6	2.3	5.3	11.1	18.1
Thistle	1.3	1.7	0.0	2.2	1.2	2.3	3.1	3.5	2.3
Flowers	6.3	5.1	8.3	5.8	5.3	11.5	12.3	16.3	18.8
Cross	1.3	0.0	0.6	1.0	1.9	5.1	5.0	10.8	11.5
OTHER MOTIFS	2.9	3.4	10.9	9.9	13.4	12.3	2.3	15.6	20.2
TOTAL NO. INVENTORIED	79	59	156	417	682	573	457	343	304
PERCENT OF GRAVESTONES WITHOUT MOTIF(S)	56	68	64	43	29	33	43	52	57

NOTE: The category 'other motifs' includes a very wide variety of decorative embellishments. The sample size inventoried is given in parentheses after each of the following motifs: scroll (45), shroud (38), crown (30), lily (25), shield (20), gate (19), masonic device (18), angel (17), anchor (16), tree (14), crucifix (13), fleur de lys (12), obelisk (11), all others (78).

Figure 1a. Illustration of clasped hands motif

(1981) singled out this sentimental Victorian zenith as the most striking feature of North American memorial practice. Ontario's post-pioneer decades certainly evoke this zenith.

Height

The height and implicit cost of gravestones made important social statements (Kephart, 1950). Obelisks soared Masai-like in the late Victorian cemetery, dwarfing the slabs around them. Often obelisks were as clustered in the cemetery as, in real life, were the prominent families they memorialized. This was especially true of Ontario's small towns and villages. Around these monumental cores, so evocative of modern downtown skyscrapers as symbols of prestige, the undulating scale and quality of other gravestones paid more subtle homage to wealth, persistence, and longevity. In this hierarchy the infant's tombstone carried the least weight and height.

The height distribution of rural Ontario gravestones changed very little between 1800 and 1869 (Table 3). The effect of peak obelisk incidence after 1880 is evident, and (as noted above) this effect persisted into the early twentieth century, albeit with fewer exceptionally tall markers.

TABLE 3. GRAVESTONE HEIGHT, RURAL ONTARIO, 1800-1909

PERIOD	NO. OF GRAVESTONES	HEIGHT IN FEET					
		One or less	Two	Three	Four	Five	Six	Seven or greater
		(percent of gravestones, row sum)						
1800-29	163	8.0	29.4	35.6	20.2	4.3	.6	1.8
1830-39	158	3.8	26.6	25.9	30.4	6.3	3.2	3.8
1840-49	363	10.2	23.4	25.3	27.3	8.5	1.4	3.9
1850-59	604	8.9	18.9	32.1	25.8	6.5	1.8	6.0
1860-69	747	10.3	19.3	32.4	23.6	5.9	2.4	6.2
1870-79	744	7.5	16.4	27.8	27.0	8.1	3.5	9.6
1880-89	806	4.9	16.4	22.7	24.8	8.4	6.5	16.2
1890-99	662	6.9	12.2	19.9	19.0	16.0	9.4	16.4
1900-09	672	8.1	10.7	16.2	22.8	22.3	10.1	9.8

Otherwise, the implicit social hierarchy based on the scale of gravestones seems to have remained remarkably stable throughout the nineteenth century in rural Ontario. Whatever relatively egalitarian standing may have characterized bush pioneers was not strikingly reflected in Ontario gravestone height in the 1830s or 1840s.

Materials

Ontario's easily worked limestones weathered rapidly. Wooden markers must have been common in pioneer settings and early family plots on farms, but have now almost all disappeared. Our survey indicates that slate slabs accounted for no more than 10 percent of markers between 1800 and 1849, and were much rarer thereafter. Limestone was used for between one half and three quarters of all surviving gravestones erected between 1800 and 1890. Sandstone was used for approximately 30 percent of markers surviving from before 1850, and 20 percent or less thereafter. Granite gravestones appeared in appreciable numbers about 1870, comprised more than a quarter of all stones erected by 1890, and the majority of new gravestones by 1900. A few white bronze monuments appear in the record. (St. Thomas, Ontario, boasted a subsidiary of the well-known Bridgeport, Connecticut, parent company.)

Orientation

The inscribed face of colonial New England vertical slabs commonly faces west; the interred *body* faces east, sandwiched between headstone and (before its later removal) footstone. Early Ontarians tended to modify this arrangement so that *both* the inscription *and* the interred remains faced east. This practice persisted (Table 4). Exceptions include rural cemeteries where stones were evidently set to face the roadside or accommodate the terrain. Gravestones 'facing' in two or more cardinal directions were of course primarily obelisks (Table 4). The eastern exposure of half or more rural Ontario gravestones *throughout* the period studied attests to the resilience of some established practices within a climate of rapid change.

TABLE 4. GRAVESTONE ORIENTATION, RURAL ONTARIO 1800-1909

PERIOD	NUMBER OF GRAVESTONES	FACING				
		East	South	West	North	Two or more Cardinal directions
		(percent of gravestones, row sum)				
1800-29	159	54.7	12.6	23.9	5.0	3.8
1830-39	152	55.3	13.8	22.4	6.6	2.0
1840-49	307	62.2	17.3	13.7	2.6	4.2
1850-59	539	60.9	14.7	16.1	4.1	4.3
1860-69	648	61.7	9.7	17.7	2.8	8.0
1870-79	673	56.5	6.7	19.0	2.4	15.5
1880-89	770	50.4	7.3	17.9	1.8	22.6
1890-99	635	48.5	6.1	16.5	2.5	26.3
1900-09	654	57.5	5.4	15.3	3.1	18.8

Manufacture

In rural Ontario cemeteries, 15 percent of pre-First World War gravestones exhibit a recognizable manufacturer's mark. This typically consists of the firm's name and its place of business, incised at the base of the gravestone. Many such marks have been obliterated by weathering, obscured by soil accumulation, or covered by a concrete base if the gravestone has been reset. Thus the *actual* incidence of manufacturer's marks was originally much higher than 15 percent. Such inscriptions were, I believe, much less common in the United States.

In Ontario, we were able to identify over 250 distinct manufacturers operating in 67 urban centers. Some marble works, such as the Hurd and Roberts company of Hamilton, distributed over a very wide area for a long period. Others were highly localized and ephemeral. Manufacturer's marks are most likely to be found on large, elaborate, or unusual monuments, on memorials shipped beyond the firm's immediate market, and in areas served by several competing firms (Norris and Krogh, 1976). The median distance gravestones were shipped was 20 miles; 10 percent of the attributed gravestones were shipped at least 75 miles from marble works to cemetery. Perhaps intensity of competition encouraged Ontario firms to label their product when circumstances warranted the practice. Some gravestones were billboards as well as memorials.

Nativity

Among 2380 gravestones for which we encoded nominal information in full as well as material-cultural characteristics, 22 percent recorded the deceased person's nativity. Nativity was most commonly reported for Ontario's first generation immigrants, especially for Irish, Scottish or German settlers. English and American Ontarians were rarely memorialized as such, and Ontario birthplaces are almost never recorded on the province's tombstones. The record of Scottish nativity typically specified the *place* of birth of the deceased, whereas Ontario Irish burials usually indicated the person's *county* of origin. This apparent tap-rootedness of the Scots and the regional identification of Ontario's Irish are, I think, a compelling example of the degree to which gravestones preserve the predilections of past society.

Case Studies

It is impossible to convey the richness and meaning of rural Ontario cemeteries solely through summary findings. Each graveyard displays a unique mix of markers, a 'signature' so to speak, based on an intertwining of local context, burial chronology, and the broader trends discussed above. The following case studies illustrate ways in which the peculiarities of local context can be understood with reference to additional sources of evidence.

Eccentric Orientation

Most nineteenth-century cemeteries achieved a replica of social ecology through the acquisition and allocation of family plots, their progressive occupancy, and placement of the dead based on marriage or kinship. These multiple ties were reinforced visually by the design and nomenclature of the monuments (Young, 1960). But rural Ontarians recognized status in, above all, the possession of land and the rootedness of families and their progeny. By these criteria, the Kitchen family had done well. Their large landholdings, near St. George, Brant County, accommodated several branches of the family by the early 1870s (Figure 2). The Kitchens were usually buried in family plots in the public cemetery north of St. George. Unlike almost all other gravestones in the cemetery, the Kitchen family memorials did not face east. Instead, the Kitchen gravestones were set facing west, toward the family's landholdings. This intriguing expression of family status was discovered in 1976 by one of my students, Miss Deborah Frame. It says much, I think, about the importance attached to family burials in past rural landscapes, and about the ability of prominent families to set, follow, or defy convention as they saw fit.

A Family Plot

Many Ontario families maintained on-farm burial grounds well into this century; some are still in use. The Shaver family cemetery, in Ancaster Township near Hamilton, Ontario, contains 43 tombstones erected since 1825. A nearby public cemetery, with over 100 markers, received its first burial in 1805. The field inventory of these two cemeteries was completed by Lynn Dilks and Sherry Bukowski in 1975. Their inventory demonstrated

FIGURE 2

Farms owned by Kitchen family, west of St. George cemetery, Ontario. All gravestones in the cemetery faced east, except the Kitchen burials, which faced west. (D. Frame, McMaster University, 1977).

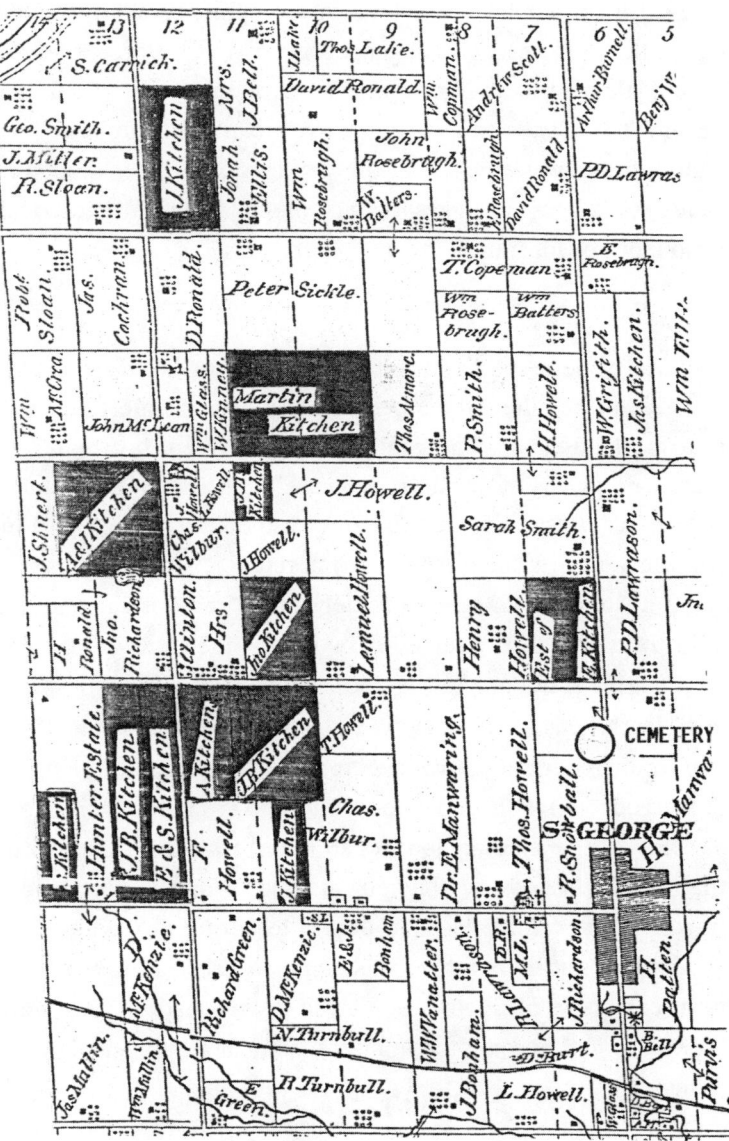

that, despite the privacy and seclusion of the Shaver family cemetery, the family's gravestones provided an outlet for innovative taste and a display of status. The first Shaver obelisk, for example, was erected in 1861, fully two decades before the first obelisk in the nearby public cemetery. The same was true of the first Shaver pulpit marker, which dates from 1888, as compared with 1923 for a similar gravestone in the public cemetery. Even the modest segmental arch vertical slab appeared two decades earlier in the family cemetery than in its public counterpart, where the first such marker was erected in 1851. Owing to the cumulative wealth and status of families which established themselves early in the Ontario landscape, their pioneer burial grounds could become showcases not of simple burial and conservative disposition, but of substance and avant-garde taste.

Deathsheds

Rural Ontario cemeteries, like the province's schoolhouses, chapels, and mills, were likely to be situated away from the postal hamlets and villages which dotted the landscape. The cemeteries were often, but by no means always, adjacent to places of worship. Because of their isolation, and often their desolation, it is easy to forget that rural cemeteries were a part of the territorial fabric which influenced social intercourse, group identity, and community life in nineteenth-century society. One can obtain some insight about the territorial role of the cemetery by linking the location of burial to the location of prior residence of the deceased (Figure 3). I call the resultant patterns "deathsheds." The examples illustrated were compiled by John Goss in 1976 from a comprehensive inventory of cemetery interments, which were then merged with a turn-of-the-century tax roll and contemporary farmers' directory. The median 'journey to burial' was less than two miles. The fact that the deathsheds overlapped was due in part to the denominational character of the cemeteries, and in part to burials of the elderly close to children who had settled nearby. This is most evident in the case of the northernmost cemetery in Figure 3, which is situated in the town of Meaford. Meaford had become the home of many of Euphrasia Township's rural offspring.

FIGURE 3

Deathsheds of twelve cemeteries serving Euphrasia Township, Grey County:
Linked Cases 1898–1914

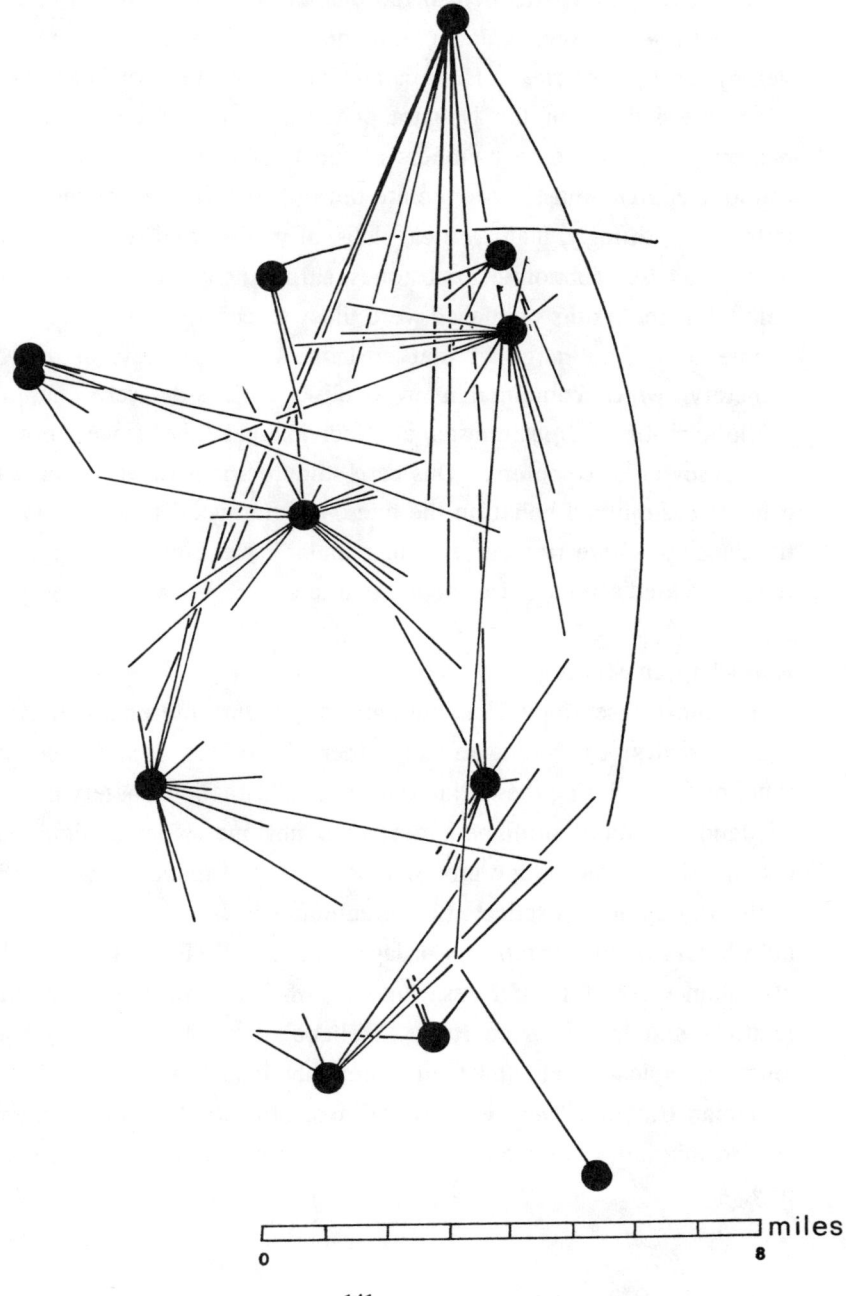

Religion

Denominational differences were not limited to *where* one was buried in rural Ontario; they extended to the memorialization of death as well. To explore these differences, Janet Hall and Marjorie Winger inventoried three nearby rural cemeteries in Haldimand County, on the shore of Lake Erie at the western limits of the Niagara peninsula. The three cemeteries were respectively confined to members of the Presbyterian church, the Roman Catholic church, and the Mennonite faith (Table 5). The memorials for the latter were, fittingly, plain vertical slabs, of modest and remarkably uniform height. These Mennonite tombstones, surprisingly, did not lack decorative detail, but the motifs employed were likely to convey a devout iconography (Table 5). The range of marker heights was greatest in the Catholic cemetery, which contained many obelisks. Crosses were the preferred Catholic motif, whereas unusual and individualized motifs were dominant in the Presbyterian cemetery. This case study demonstrates not only the imprint of custom and belief on the micro-geography of the cemetery, but also the dangers of inferring currents of popular taste from small or denominationally biased samples of cemetery markers.

Ethnicity and Status

The next case study illustrates group-specific differences in gravestone characteristics, controlling for any other differences accountable to place, time, or faith. Using the burial register of a Catholic cemetery in the city of Welland, as well as surname and other tombstone evidence, Paula Esposito distinguished three ethnic groups among 77 interments between 1890 and 1919. Italian burials reflected a community which had formed after the establishment of the Plymouth Cordage Works in Welland, and its relocation of Italian workers from Massachusetts, who then prompted migration of relatives and friends from Italy. Welland's turn-of-the-century Slavic immigrants typically held low-paid commonly industrial jobs. The British-Canadian Catholics were well established, often Irish, many of them traceable to migratory labor on the Welland Canal in the early nineteenth century.

TABLE 5

Denominational differences in motif preference:
Three cemeteries in Haldimand County, Ontario, 1870 - 1899

MOTIFS	RELIGION		
	PRESBYTERIAN	MENNONITE	CATHOLIC
	(Percent of gravestones)		
Willow	--	5.1	--
Hand of God	--	1.3	--
Clasped Hands	--	16.7	--
Bible	8.3	14.1	--
Lamb	8.3	7.7	4.2
Flowers, Wreaths	12.5	23.1	--
Cross, Crucifix	--	--	54.1
All other motifs	41.7	23.1	16.7
NO MOTIF PRESENT	29.2	9.0	25.0
TOTAL	100.0	100.0	100.0

SOURCE: J. Hall and M. Winger, McMaster University, 1976; based on field inventory of 174 gravestones.

The different footholds these groups had achieved within Welland society are apparent from the memorials to their dead (Table 6). In particular, the British-Canadians were more likely to pay for decorative motifs, more able to afford obelisks (or, failing those, granite blocks), and judging from the mix of lettering employed, more inclined to combine prominently displayed raised family names with incised biographical detail. The Italian markers are mostly plain limestone slabs with a brief inscription and little or no decorative detail. The Slavic markers are no larger than the Italian gravestones, but are more varied in form, more decorative, and durable. Ms. Esposito's study illustrates the interdependence of cultural and socioeconomic factors in the material expression of ethnic groups as successive waves of immigrants entered Ontario between the late eighteenth century and the First World War.

TABLE 6
Ethnicity and Status: The Japanese Martyrs' Catholic Cemetery,
Welland, Ontario, 1890 – 1919

GRAVESTONE ATTRIBUTE	ETHNICITY		
	ITALIAN	BRITISH	EASTERN EUROPEAN
	(percent of gravestones associated with ethnic group)		
HEIGHT			
greater than 4 feet	—	33	—
MATERIAL			
granite markers	26	44	39
LETTERING			
Incised and raised	4	22	—
MOTIF			
Motif present	18	39	26
VERTICAL SLAB FORM			
Non-rectangular design	40	64	67

SOURCE: P. Esposito, McMaster University, 1975

Diffusion and Context

Were remote regions and isolated localities slow to adopt new styles? Eastern Grey County remained unsettled until the 1840s, yet its adoption of the tablet marker is scarcely distinguishable from the advent and peak popularity of this form in our overall sample (Table 7, compare Table 1). Moreover, Eastern Grey shunned this form quite early, whereas the tablet marker persisted in isolated rural graveyards within 20 miles of Hamilton, the province's second largest city (Table 7). In the *villages* around Hamilton, however, the tablet marker was already widely in use by the 1860s (Table 7). This was a full decade before the tablet's peak popularity in Pennsylvania (Hannon, 1973), and two decades before its peak in Francaviglia's Wisconsin survey, and fully three decades before its zenith in rural Oregon (Francaviglia, 1971). These results should not mislead the reader into assuming that the diffusion of gravestone taste was a broad east-to-west spread, qualified by pockets of urbane innovation and stolid resistance. I am convinced that the answer to these regional and contextual variations lies primarily in modes of manufacture, pricing, and distribution, not in patterns of taste. Detailed studies of the records of Victorian marble works are needed to explore these questions.

Conclusion

I trust that this essay has helped to dispel the perception that Victorian gravestones have little to compel our interest or study. Granted, nineteenth-century rural Ontario was no showpiece for the independent carver. Nor were its cemeteries enriched by the large tombs or memorial art that can be found in urban necropolises throughout the United States and Canada. Rural aspirations rarely went beyond what could be cut, shipped, and erected for a reasonable price. Thus status after death was free of the more flagrant excesses of old money and the nouveau riche in cities. In any case, by these standards, rural Ontarians were neither wealthy nor inclined to conspicuous display.

What emerges from this survey of form, decorative detail, and other gravestone characteristics is a sense of rural Ontarian conservatism unwilling or unable to take full advantage of the repertoire of choice offered by

TABLE 7

Tablet (Round-headed) Marker Incidence in Three Ontario Settings, 1850 – 1909

DECADE	SETTING		
	URBAN MARGINS	URBAN MARGINS	PIONEER FRINGE
	Village Graveyards near Hamilton	Isolated Graveyards near Hamilton	Grey County
	(Tablets as percent of all gravestones)		
1850s	6.8	1.2	3.7
1860s	36.5	8.7	13.0
1870s	39.6	35.8	30.9
1880s	32.1	18.7	22.6
1890s	21.7	13.5	1.6
1900s	10.0	8.7	—

NOTE: Grey County's pioneer settlement phase generally spanned the period 1840–1865; the Hamilton area was settled between 1790 and 1825.

SOURCE: Field inventory, McMaster University, 1975–77; 201 tablet markers were sampled in 28 cemeteries.

Victorian marble works. It was not until the 1870s that the earmarks of popular culture were fully evident in the Ontario cemetery. It is, I think, noteworthy that Ontario's rural domestic architecture exhibits much the same hesitancy; Gothic was more a matter of cheap adornment than design before the 1870s, and Italianate villas were likewise largely a post-Confederation phenomenon. Yet Ontarians did not perpetuate a Loyalist tradition in memorial art any more than they continued to erect Loyalist homes. Moreover, their material culture exhibited very little that could confidently be termed Scots or Irish. In the matter of gravestones, houses, barns, fences, and other trappings of the cultural landscape early Ontarians exhibited a remarkable ability to achieve distinctiveness through selectivity, adaptation, and stubborn adherence to 'norms' which had little or nothing to do with their ancestry. Their imprint is still evident, a middle landscape between folk-based homogeneity and vacillating currents of popular taste. Their graveyards are very much a part of this imprint.

Acknowledgments

I wish to thank Mrs. Sharron Paulman of S.U.N.Y. Geneseo for her invaluable assistance in deriving final results from the Ontario gravestone computer file. The coding of the records was supported by the Canada Council in 1978-79, and undertaken by Randy Widdis and Cheryl Hall Hoffman at McMaster University. Their ability to decipher and make sense of the original inventory forms was a crucial step in this research. I also wish to acknowledge the work of Victor Konrad, a 1975 graduate colleague at McMaster who collaborated in the design and early trials of our standard inventory form. And of course without the hundred or so McMaster student volunteers this survey could not have been completed. My work on gravestone analysis had been in abeyance for four years when I joined the A.G.S. Thanks to the members for their encouragement, most especially Pat Miller and Gaynell Stone. Thanks too to the Cooperstown N.Y.S.H.A. seminarians and staff who rekindled my enthusiasm for cemetery research. My patient and congenial secretary, Mrs. Loretta Stratton, coped with the assorted, often chaotic, drafts of this essay, and as always produced a fine typescript.

REFERENCES CITED

ARIES, Phillipe, *The Hour of Our Death*, (New York: Alfred A. Knopf, 1981).

BENES, Peter, *The Masks of Orthodoxy*, (Amherst, MA: University of Massachusetts Press, 1977).

DARDEN, J.T., "Factors in the Location of Pittsburgh Cemeteries," *The Virginia Geographer* (1972), Vol. 7, pp. 3-8.

DETHLEFSEN, E., and J. DEETZ, "Death's Heads, Cherubs, and Willow Trees: Experimental Archaeology in Colonial Cemeteries," *American Antiquity* (1966), Vol. 31, pp. 502-10.

FRANCAVIGLIA, Richard V., "The Cemetery as an Evolving Cultural Landscape," *Annals* (The Association of American Geographers, 1971) Vol. 61 (3), pp. 501-9.

HALL, Roger, and Bruce BOWDEN, "Beautifying the Boneyard: The Changing Image of the Cemetery in Nineteenth-Century Ontario," *Material History Bulletin*, (1986), Vol. 23, Spring, pp. 13-24.

HANKS, Carole, *Early Ontario Gravestones*, (Toronto: McGraw Hill Ryerson Ltd., 1974).

HANNON, T.J., "Nineteenth Century Cemeteries in Central West Pennsylvania," *Proceedings*, (The Pioneer America Society, 1973), Vol. 2, pp. 23-8.

JEANE, Donald G., "A Plea for the End of Tombstone-Style Geography," *Annals*, (The Association of American Geographers, 1972), Vol. 62, No. 1, pp. 146-148.

JEANE, D. Gregory, "The Upland South Cemetery: An American Type," *Journal of Popular Culture* (1978), Vol. 11, No. 4, pp. 895-903.

KEPHART, W., "Status After Death," *American Sociological Review* (1950), Vol. 15, pp. 635-43.

KNIFFEN, Fred, "Necrogeography in the United States," *Geographical Review* (1967), Vol. 57, pp. 426-7.

KNIGHT, David. B., "Cemeteries as Living Landscapes," (Ontario Genealogical Society, Ottawa Branch, Publication 73-8, 1973).

LUDWIG, Allan, *Graven Images*, (Middletown, CT: Wesleyan University Press, 1966).

NORRIS, Darrell A., and Anne KROGH, "Cemetery Marker Origin: A Key to Market Evolution," in Darrell A. Norris and Victor Konrad, Eds. *Visible Landscapes of the Past*, (Department of Geography, McMaster University, 1976).

OSBORNE, Brian S., "The Cemeteries of the Midland District of Upper Canada: A Note on Mortality in a Frontier Society," *Pioneer America*, (1974) Vol. 6, pp. 46-55.

PATTERSON, Nancy-Lou, "The Iron Cross and The Tree of Life: German-Alsatian Gravemarkers in Waterloo Region and Bruce County Roman Catholic Cemeteries," *Ontario History*, (1976), Vol. 48, No. 1, pp. 1-16.

PIKE, Martha V., and Janice Gray ARMSTRONG, *A Time to Mourn: Expressions of Grief in Nineteenth Century America*, (The Museums at Stony Brook, Stony Brook, NY, 1980).

STONE, Patricia, and Lynn RUSSELL, "Observation on Figures, Human and Divine, on Nineteenth-Century Ontario Gravestones," *Material History Bulletin* (1986), Vol. 24, Fall, pp. 23-29.

TASHJIAN, Dickran, and Ann TASHJIAN, *Memorials for Children of Change: The Art of*

Early New England Stonecarving, (Middletown, CT: Wesleyan University Press, 1974).

WALLACE, William D., *B.H. Kinney, 1821-1888: Gravestone Carver and Sculptor*, (Worcester Historical Museum, Worcester, MA, 1985).

YOUNG, Frank W., "Graveyards and Social Structure," *Rural Sociology*, (1960), Vol. 25 (4), pp. 446-50.

ZELINSKY, Wilbur, "Unearthy Delights: Cemetery Names and the Map of the Changing American Afterworld," in David Lowenthal and Martyn Bowden, Eds., *Geographies of the Mind*, (New York: Oxford Unversity Press, 1975).

Springbrook Farm, Grey County, Ontario

Map of Kings County, Nova Scotia (circa 1818)

RESEARCH REPORT ON THE GRAVEYARDS OF KINGS COUNTY, NOVA SCOTIA*

Deborah Trask and Debra McNabb

In Nova Scotia most of what is known about life in the late eighteenth and early nineteenth centuries has been gleaned from scant documents -- diaries, newspapers, correspondence, wills, deeds -- and the story they tell is far from complete. To understand more of this period, we have begun to investigate Nova Scotia gravestones, combining artifact information with historical records, thereby relating material, maker and location of the stones with what is known about the people they memorialize and the communities in which those people lived. This report discusses the findings of research to date.

A cursory examination of the old graveyards of Nova Scotia reveals that gravestones pre-dating 1780 are generally made of slate, ornately carved in the style common around Massachusetts Bay, and in fact, imported from there.[1] Between 1780 and 1840 most stones were made locally by Nova Scotian craftsmen and can be grouped by area, according to common characteristics of material and style. For the most part, Halifax stones were carved in sandstone in very high relief by Scottish stone masons who originally came to the capital to construct public buildings. A few stones of this style can also be found in the major towns nearest to Halifax -- Windsor and Lunenburg -- where they stand alongside more primitive local carving of the same period. From Liverpool to Yarmouth there are imported New

---

* This report originally appeared, in a slightly different form, in *Material History Bulletin* 23 (Spring 1986) published by the History Division of the Canadian Museum of Civilization in Ottawa, and is printed here with the kind permission of the editor of the *Bulletin*. The authors wish to emphasize that this is to be read as an overview of work in progress. We hope that their project will be extended to include research in the New York area for evidence of the sources of Seaman's work, a scouring of North Cumberland County for further examples of the work of the Horton Carvers, and a geological analysis which will pinpoint the sources of their material.

England slates (more common and of later date), a few Halifax sandstones, and an obvious "south shore" style of crude carving on local scaly schist.[2] Throughout Cape Breton, as well as Pictou and Antigonish Counties, eighteenth- and very early nineteenth-century stones are uncommon, but those that survive are usually sandstone and of formal design. In Cumberland and Colchester Counties there are also few early gravestones, and their style is more folksy. Around the Annapolis River the old stones tend to be sandstone carved in a style popular along the Saint John River, just across the Bay of Fundy. In Kings County, Nova Scotia, another distinctly identifiable carving style can be found. There are more than 100 stones in this style -- a remarkable number compared with other rural areas. This concentration is attributable perhaps not so much to survival as to the fact that this was one of the first English-speaking areas of the province to develop a local economy which could support a resident gravestone carver.

Our research to date has focused on that area of Kings County, Nova Scotia, which was set off in the 1750s as the townships of Horton and Cornwallis. These townships were settled in the early 1760s as part of a campaign by the Nova Scotia government to attract New Englanders to the colony. Just a few years before, and after almost one hundred and fifty years of habitation, the colony's resident French Acadian population had been forcibly deported and the land lay empty. Between 1760 and 1764 more than 5000 New Englanders took up grants of free land ranging from 250 to 1000 acres in eleven townships of approximately 100,000 acres each, located along Nova Scotia's southwestern shore, the Annapolis Valley, the Minas Basin and the isthmus of Chignecto.

Prospective immigrants from the land-hungry agricultural areas of New England were especially interested in the fertile alluvial farmland in the heart of Acadia at Les Mines (Minas). The Nova Scotia government partitioned this land as the townships of Cornwallis, Horton and Falmouth. These townships were to be colonized as block settlements, i.e. each was granted to a group of families and individuals who were expected to move from New England to Nova Scotia as a community and to occupy the land, at least initially, in common. But as the colonization proceeded, forfeitures, vacancies and the influx of non-grantees led to the settlement of the Minas townships by a diverse group of proprietors. In Horton, for example, three components can be recognized in the final selection of grantees: 177 New Englanders, 14 soldiers and 11 placemen.[3] Still, most of the grantees - perhaps 88% - were New Englanders. Male grantees ranged in age between 15 and 66, more than two-thirds were married and brought between one and ten, but most often four, children under age 21 to the new land. Many families included one or two sons aged 16 to 21 who were not grantees and could labor on family farms.

Little of the economic background of the New England settlers can be known without reconstructing their lives prior to emigration. While it is very unlikely that the extremely rich or the very poor came to Kings County, the sparse evidence suggests that the grantees represented a broad economic spectrum. For instance, such men as prominent Connecticut landowner Robert Denison, Yale-educated lawyer Nathan Dewolf, and Col. Charles Dickson (who personally financed a military company for the siege of Beausejour) came to Horton, but other settlers could not survive the first few years without food and grain subsidies from the Nova Scotia government. Although almost every man called himself a yeoman farmer when he claimed a Horton share, the New Englanders brought a variety of skills to the new land. A small number identified themselves as blacksmiths, carpenters, cordwainers, weavers and traders, while others relied on informal training to build their houses and provide their families with the basic possessions they had not brought with them.

If the origins of the 79 New Englanders who settled in Horton for whom we have data are typical, members of this largest group of grantees came from a compact area of southeastern Connecticut focusing on the port of New London and including the towns of Lebanon, Colchester, Norwich, East Haddam, Lyme and Stonington. A few others came from communities along the Connecticut River.

The gravestones which still stand in Horton as memorials to these New Englanders are different from those found in their hearth areas. In southeastern Connecticut mid-eighteenth-century gravestones are mainly granite, with shallow carved angel-head motifs (soul effigies) predominantly the work of Benjamin Collins, the Manning family and their imitators.[4] This style of carving contrasts sharply with the ornate and deeply incised sandstones of the Connecticut River Valley. Both major Connecticut carving styles differ considerably from the slate carving styles of Massachusetts and Rhode Island.[5] In fact, the gravestones of Kings County, Nova Scotia, bear little resemblance to those found anywhere in New England from the mid-eighteenth century.[6]

The oldest Kings County gravestones date from about 1770 to 1820. The earliest are probably "back-dated" -- carved some time later than the date indicated on the stone. From the evidence of the stones, there does not appear to have been anyone carving gravestones in Horton before the 1780s. The oldest markers appear to be primarily the creation of two stonecarvers, working exclusively in sandstone. The first is referred to as the "Second Horton Carver" because his name is unknown and he succeeded an earlier carver who worked only briefly in the area.[7] The second has been identified as Abraham Seaman. These attributions have been made following a systematic investigation of the older burial grounds in Nova Scotia. Pre-1830 stones were closely scrutinized and grouped in terms of material, shape, lettering, image, border, word groupings, and any other visibly identifiable characteristics. Probate records were then studied for any reference to individuals paid to carve gravestones. This kind of information is rarely noted in estate settlement papers. Not every death involved an estate settlement (especially those of young men, children and many women), and not all probate records have survived. Thus the identity of the Second Horton Carver remains a mystery.

Stones attributed to the Second Horton Carver date from 1798 to 1805 (Appendix A).[8] He carved crude, sad faces with an elaborate carved "rope" edge and vining or "bird-track" border. His earliest stones have deep outlines around the winged-head image, or no image at all and a plain curved shape at the top edge (Fig. 1). Later the top edge shape became more elaborate and he added a plain or beaded bracket around the "Here Lies" part of the inscription (Fig. 2). There is also a further cutting away above the head, and often the epitaph "Death is a debt that is nature's due,/Which I have paid and so must you." He never mastered the depiction of hair. A curious distinguishing mark of the Second Horton Carver is a tail on the

Fig. 1. Benjamin Peck stone, sandstone, 1801, Kentville, Kings County, N.S. Attributed carver: Second Horton carver, first style. Photo by Dan and Jessie Lie Farber.

Fig. 2. Eunice Harris stone, sandstone, 1803, Upper Canard, Kings County, N.S. Attributed carver: Second Horton carver, second style. Photo by Deborah Trask.

Fig. 3. James C. & Thomas Griffin stone, sandstone, 1810, Kentville, Kings County, N.S. Attributed carver: Abraham Seaman. Photo by Dan and Jessie Lie Farber.

Fig. 4. Henry Magee stone, sandstone, 1806, Kentville, Kings County, N.S. Attributed carver: Abraham Seaman. Photo by Dan and Jessie Lie Farber.

crossbar of the "f" in "Here lies the body of." Stones with these characteristics are found in all the old burial grounds of Cornwallis and Horton, with some at nearby Falmouth and Windsor. A few stones for former residents of Horton have been discovered outside the area. There is one for Charles Dickson at St. Paul's Cemetery in Halifax, and another for Susannah, wife of Nathan Harris, at Liverpool.

Field investigation has revealed a second style of carving on stones dated from 1805 to 1821 (Appendix B).[9] This carver also used the elaborate carved "rope" edge, the vining or "bird-track" border, and added a swirl to the crossbar on the "f" in "In Memory of," but he executed these decorations with greater dexterity (Figs. 3 & 4). He generally carved the name of the deceased in capital letters. His technique is undoubtedly derived from the earlier style, for there is a clear visible link between the two. He may have learned the trade of stonecarving from the Second Horton Carver. It is quite possible that this carver and the Second Horton Carver are the same person, and these stylistic variations show the evolution of carving skill in one craftsman.[10]

Documentary evidence identifies this carving as the work of Abraham Seaman. Probate estate papers for three decedents whose stones have these characteristics record payments to Abraham Seaman for gravestones (Figs. 5, 6 & 7 a,b).[11] Seaman is also mentioned in the journal of Edward Manning, minister of the First Baptist Church in Cornwallis. On April 30, 1818, six weeks after his daughter Eunice died, Manning recorded: "Saw Mr. Abraham Seamans, presented bill for Eunice's gravestone, 6 pounds, 4 shillings, but he deducted 1 pound 4 shillings."[12]

Abraham Seaman was the son of Jacomiah Seaman of Westchester, New York.[13] During the American Revolution, Jacomiah's four sons joined Col. Lowther Pennington's Regiment of Kings Guards, and so became members of the group known as the Westchester Loyalists.[14] After the war many Westchester Loyalists received land grants in Cumberland County, Nova Scotia. Jacomiah and his son Stephen each received a 500-acre grant at "Cobequid Road," Cumberland County, and later were granted a second tract near River Philip.[15] Jacomiah probably settled in the township of Fanningsborough (now North Wallace).[16] In 1788 his son Abraham "of the

Fig. 5. Thomas Miner stone, sandstone, 1801, Wolfville, Kings County, N.S. Attributed carver: Abraham Seaman. Photo by Deborah Trask.

Fig. 6. Rachel Fitch stone, sandstone, 1808, Wolfville, Kings County, N.S., tympanum detail. Attributed carver: Abraham Seaman. Photo by Deborah Trask.

7a.

7b.

Figs. 7 a,b. Ezekiel Woodworth stone, sandstone, 1812, Chipman's Corner, Kings County, N.S. Probated carver: Abraham Seaman. Photo by Deborah Trask.

township of Westchester, County of Cumberland, yeoman" bought 50 acres on the north side of the main road leading from Amherst to Cobequid (Truro), which he sold less than two years later.[17] In October 1794, at the age of twenty-four, Abraham Seaman of Westmoreland, Cumberland County, bought a house and a one-acre lot in Horton.[18] The following year he married into a prominent Horton family and lived there until 1821, when he moved back to Cumberland County.[19]

In the intervening years, Abraham Seaman had amassed considerable land holdings in Cumberland County. In 1802, Abraham Seaman "of Horton, Kings County, merchant," bought some land at River Philip. In September of 1806 he bought an additional 1000 acres at River Philip, and the next month, listed now as a mason, he bought some more land in Horton. Years later, while helping his brother Stephen settle a land dispute at River Philip (now Pugwash), he swore that "...in 1806 I went from Horton to Pugwash Built a House on the West side of Pugwash harbour the first there ever..."[20] But, as far as we know, he continued to live at Horton. In March of 1811 he bought dykeland at Horton; in October of the same year he bought five tracts of land including a half interest in a sawmill at River Philip from his brother Hezekiah. On all of these deeds he is listed as being "of Horton."[21]

As a landowner, merchant and mason, Seaman was probably involved in a variety of business activities during the time he lived in Horton. One of his most enduring activities was making distinctive gravestones for his neighbors. At least part of the reason Seaman's stones have survived is because of the material he used. His stones are a high-quality, dense brown sandstone that seems out of place in a settlement bordering the Bay of Fundy. It bears little resemblance to the material used by his son, Thomas Lewis Seaman, when he made gravestones in Kings County during the 1830s and 40s.[22] The younger Seaman relied more on a porous, reddish sandstone which seems to be characteristic of the Minas Basin area. The stone has succumbed over time to water damage, and has become very crumbly. The superior material used by Abraham Seaman is more like the stone found at Remsheg (Wallace), Cumberland County. Stone from the Remsheg quarry was used to build Province House in Halifax, which was finished before

1819. The architect Richard Scott bought the land on the Remsheg River which included the stone quarries in 1814.[23] The deed implies that the quarries had been worked previously, but precisely when sandstone was first quarried there is as yet unknown. If sandstone was being transported from Remsheg to Halifax, could it also have gone to the Horton-Cornwallis district? We know that the house built for Charles Ramage Prescott in Cornwallis township, completed before 1817, has a sandstone foundation and lintels. Although the brick for the house was made nearby,[24] the source for the sandstone has not been ascertained. We do not know if Seaman had access to Wallace sandstone. Until the early Kings County gravestones are analyzed by a geologist, conclusions about the source of Seaman's sandstone are tenuous at best.

Still, if Seaman transported his raw material from north Cumberland to Kings County, this would reveal patterns of trade and perceptions of distance and travel in turn-of-the-nineteenth-century Nova Scotia. Undoubtedly Seaman himself traveled this route regularly to maintain his family and business connections in Cumberland County.

In addition to material, maker and origins of the people for whom they were made, the gravestones were examined in the context of the lives these people lived in Horton. An analysis of the stones according to origin, religion and place of residence of the decedents, their economic standing within the group of founding settlers, and kinship ties to each other and to Abraham Seaman reveals that the only connection most share is the timing of their arrival in Horton. Almost all extant stones for the period 1770 to 1820 for this area of Kings County commemorate the township's grantees. Few exist for those who took up residence after all the land in the township had been granted, even though this group represented a significant component of the population. Between 1770 and 1791 at least 177 men and their families became residents of Horton.[25]

In that time, restricted access to land resulting from land granting policies, the accumulative impulses of a handful of the largest landowners, rising prices and increased pressure of population lessened everyman's opportunity to own a farm. As a result, few latecomers ever acquired land. For the most part they rented property or labored on someone else's farm.

There were few alternatives in this subsistence farming community. Almost immediately, society stratified on the basis of land ownership. Thus when Hortonians were finally laid to rest, it was those who had taken part in the initial settling and had obtained free land grants who were in a position to have gravestones erected in their memory.

The carver of these gravestones was a native of Westchester, New York, and not of New England and thus his cultural traditions may have been different from those of the people whose memorials he carved. He did not settle immediately in Kings County when he came to Nova Scotia, and the fact that he may have transported the material for his work from the area where he first lived (and continued to own property) raises some questions about why he moved to Horton. In eighteenth and early nineteenth century New England, carvers usually lived near a stone quarry.[26] When Abraham Seaman began carving in Horton, it was the shire town of the most populated county in the colony (except Halifax) and the first generation of settlers was dying. Had he deliberately located close to his market?[27]

Like the Cape Cod cottages and Georgian houses that dot the countryside, the old gravestones of Kings County *seem* to be part of the New England cultural traditions that are stamped on the landscape. As we begin to examine these artifacts more closely, it is clear that the story they tell is more complex. Although more research has to be done in this regard, it appears that gravestones were carved by Abraham Seaman in a style distinctive to Nova Scotia.

Appendix A

Gravestones attributed to the Second Horton Carver.

First style:

Jane Chipman	1775	Chipman's Corner
Nathaniel Thomas	1787	Windsor
Asa Wickwire	1795	"Factory Cemetery", near Jawbone Corner
Charles Dickson	1796	Halifax - St. Paul's Cemetery
Ann Blackmore	1797	Onslow
Lucy Haliburton	1797	Windsor

Hannah Best	1798	Kentville
Joseph Chase Jr.	1798	Upper Canard
Charlotte Curry	1799	Chipman's Corner
Handley Chipman	1799	Chipman's Corner
Eliza Wells	1800	Upper Canard
Joseph Chase	1801	Upper Canard
Nathan Rand	1801	Wolfville
Lucretia Rogers	1801	Wolfville
Benjamin Peck	1801	Kentville
Sabra Peck	1801	Kentville

Second style:

Stephen Post	1768	Chipman's Corner
Margaret Ratchford	1794	Parrsboro
Mary Forsyth	1796	Wolfville
Lydia Fitch	1797	Simpson's Bridge, Maple Street
William Northup	1800	Falmouth
William Freeman	1801	West Amherst
Anna Fitch	1802	Simpson's Bridge, Maple Street
Martha Harris	1802	Upper Canard
Nancy Chipman	1802	Chipman's Corner
Gilbert Forsyth	1802	Wolfville
James Duncanson	1802	Wolfville
Eunice Harris	1803	Upper Canard
Ann Bishop	1803	Wolfville
Caroline Bishop	1803	Wolfville
Susannah Harris	1803	Liverpool
Perry Borden	1805	Upper Canard
Samuel Reed	1805	Wolfville

Appendix B

Stones attributed to Abraham Seaman:

Sarah Whidden	1779	Truro
Simeon Porter	1779	Chipman's Corner
Mercy Bishop	1783	Wolfville
John Bishop	1785	Wolfville
Mary Benjamin	1786	Wolfville
Silas Woodworth	1790	Chipman's Corner
George Oxley	179?	River Philip (broken)
Silvanus Miner	1794	Wolfville
Thomas Watson	1796	West Amherst
William Alline	1799	Wolfville
Ann Miner	1801	Wolfville
Thomas Miner	1801	Wolfville
William Griffin	1802	Fox Hill Cem., Cornwallis
Margaret Brown	1803	Wolfville

Name	Year	Location
Mathew Dickie	1803	Chipman's Corner
Edward Church	1804	Windsor
Stephen Sheffield	1805	Upper Canard
Elizabeth Tonge	1805	Windsor
Isaac Deschamps	1805	Windsor
Joshua T. De St. Croix	1805	Bridgetown
Obed Benjamin	1806	Wolfville
Henry Magee	1806	Kentville
Patrick Murray	1806	Kentville
John Dickie	1807	Chipman's Corner
Mary Deck	1808	Kentville
Rachel Fitch	1808	Wolfville
Rebecca Alline	1808	Wolfville
Mary Bishop	1808	Simpson's Bridge, Maple St.
Sarah Woodworth	1808	Chipman's Corner
James C./Thomas Giffin	1810	Kentville
William Skene	1810	Fox Hill Cem., Cornwallis
Barnabus Lord	1810	Chipman's Corner
Jarusha Dickey	1810	Chipman's Corner
Elias Tupper	1810	Chipman's Corner
Jonathan Shearman	1810	Upper Canard
Betsy Morton	1810	Gagetown N.B.
William/Ann Dunkin	1811/07	River Philip
Catherine Simpson	1811	St. Paul's Cem., Halifax
*Cyrus Peck	1812	Kentville
Lutitia Reed	1812	Upper Canard
Samuel Gore	1812	Wolfville
*Ezekiel Woodworth	1812	Chipman's Corner
Benjamin Jarvis	1812	Church of St. John, Church Street
John/Elizabeth Burbidge	1812	Fox Hill Cem., Cornwallis
John Palmeter	1812	"Factory Cemetery", near Jaw Bone Corner
Daniel Wood	1813	Upper Canard
Polly Chipman	1813	Chipman's Corner
Thomas Ratchford	1813	Wolfville
Dester Ratchford	1813	Wolfville
Hannah Chase	1815	Upper Canard
Jinnat Dickie	1815	Chipman's Corner
Mercury Cumming	1815	Chipman's Corner
*John Bishop	1815	Simpson's Bridge, Maple Street
Thomas H. Woodward	1815	Wolfville
Holmes Cogswell	1815	Upper Canard
Henry Burbidge	1815?	Fox Hill Cem., Cornwallis
Captain Mason Cogswell	1816	Chipman's Corner
Levena Bishop	1816	Wolfville
Susannah Starr	1817	Starr's Point
Samuel Tupper	1817	Chipman's Corner
John Turner	1817	Wolfville
Rebekah Cumming	1817	Chipman's Corner
Sarah Dickie	1817	Chipman's Corner
Thomas Woodworth	1817	Upper Canard

*Eunice Manning	1818	Upper Canard
Elizabeth Barnaby	1818	Chipman's Corner
Eunice Forsyth	1819	Wolfville
George Reid	1820	Wolfville
Abijah Pearson	1820	Upper Canard
*Timothy Barnaby	1820	Chipman's Corner
Eunice Hamilton	1820	Grand Pre
John/Cynthy Moss	1821/20	Wolfville
Deborah Cottnam	n.d.	Windsor
Rebeka Nisbet	n.d.	Chipman's Corner
Mary Calkin	n.d.	Simpson's Bridge, Maple Street
Jeremiah Calkin	n.d.	Simpson's Bridge, Maple Street
Isaac Graham	n.d.	Wolfville
Thomas Stevens	n.d.	Wolfville

* stones known to have been carved by Abraham Seaman.

NOTES

1. Deborah E. Trask, *Life How Short, Eternity How Long, Gravestone Carving and Carvers in Nova Scotia* (Halifax: Nova Scotia Museum, 1978) p. 10-14.
2. Deborah E. Trask. "The South Shore Carver", *The Occasional* Vol. 9 #2, Nova Scotia Museum, 1985.
3. For information on the settlement of Horton, see Debra A. McNabb, "Land and Families in Horton Township", unpublished M.A. thesis, University of British Columbia, 1986.
4. We are indebted to Dr. James Slater, of Mansfield CT, and the Association for Gravestone Studies for identifying carving styles in southeastern Connecticut, and to Susan Kelly and Anne Williams, also of AGS, for their assistance in checking gravestones in Old Lyme and New London. In relation to this project, the authors have investigated graveyards in Mansfield Center, Lebanon (Trumbull), Columbia and Windham, Connecticut. For specific information on Connecticut gravestone carving, see a series of articles by Dr. Ernest Caulfield published in the *Connecticut Historical Society Bulletin* between 1951 and 1967, continued by Peter Benes and James Slater from Dr. Caulfield's research, 1975-1983, particularly: "Connecticut Gravestones VIII", (Vol. 27 #3, July 1962) on the Manning family; "Connecticut Gravestones IX" (Vol. 28 #1, January 1963) on the Collins family; "Connecticut Gravestones XIII" (Vol. 40 #2, April 1975) on the Kimball family; and "Connecticut Gravestones XV" (Vol. 43 #1, January 1978) on three Manning imitators.
5. To reduce the stylistic trends of gravestone carving in eighteenth-century New England to three regional styles is a gross oversimplification. For purposes of this paper, this is adequate, but for more information on New England gravestone carving, the main texts are: Harriette M. Forbes, *Gravestones of Early New England and the Men Who Made Them, 1653-1800* (Boston, MA: Houghton Mifflin, 1927); Alan I. Ludwig, *Graven Images* (Middletown CT: Wesleyan University Press, 1968); Dickran and Anne Tashjian, *Memorials for Children of Change* (Middletown CT: Wesleyan University Press, 1975); Peter Benes, *The Masks of Orthodoxy* (Amherst MA: University of Massachusetts Press, 1977).
6. A comparison of Connecticut and Kings County carving styles can be found in the old Cornwallis township burial ground at Chipman's Corner, Kings County, Nova Scotia where there stands a signed Connecticut sandstone (Chester Kimball, New London) dated 1785, among the locally carved stones.

7. Trask, *Life How Short*, "The Horton Carver" p. 18-19.
8. Ibid., "The Second Horton Carver" p. 20-21.
9. Ibid., "The Seaman Family" p. 71-73.
10. We have considered that Abraham Seaman's father, Jacomiah, who was a mason (see footnote 16), might have been the Second Horton Carver, but there is no evidence that he ever carved gravestones, nor any indication that he was ever in Horton.
11. Kings County Probate Records, Public Archives of Nova Scotia, RG 48. Estates of Timothy Barnaby, 1821 ("pd Abr^m Simmons for Grave Stones L5"); John Bishop, 1815 "paid Abram Seamans 7.0.0"); Cyrus Peck 1812 ("paid Mr. Abraham Seaman Acct in full L4.14.-"); Ezekiel Woodworth, 1812 ("To Abraham Seamans for Grave Stones L3.10.-").
12. Journal of Edward Manning, in Special Collections, Vaughan Memorial Library, Acadia University, Wolfville, Nova Scotia, courtesy of Dr. B.M. Moody.
13. A.W.H. Eaton, *History of Kings County* (Salem, Mass.: Salem Press, 1910), p. 814-5.
14. James F. Smith, *The History of Pugwash* (Pugwash, N.S.: North Cumberland Historical Society, publication #8, 1978), p. 3.
15. Marion Gilroy, *Loyalists and Land Settlement in Nova Scotia* (Halifax: Public Archives of Nova Scotia, publication #4, 1937), p. 41.
16. "I, Jacomiah Seaman of the township of Fannings Burrow and County of Cumberland, Mason..." Cumberland County Estate Papers, Public Archives of Nova Scotia (PANS) RG 48, estate of Jacomiah Seaman, probated August 8, 1808.
17. Cumberland County Deeds (PANS RG 47) Book D, p. 80 and p. 193.
18. Kings County Deeds (PANS RG 47) Book 4, p. 265.
19. Day Book of Timothy Bishop (1740-1827, Abraham Seaman's father-in-law) covering 1775-1824, (PANS MG 3) "Abraham Seaman moved to Pugwash November 27, 1821."
20. Sworn statement of Abraham Seaman, 1827, quoted in Smith, *History of Pugwash*, p. 9.
21. Cumberland County Deeds (PANS RG 47) Book F, p. 44, p. 190, p. 334; Kings County Deeds Book 5, p. 218; Book 6, p. 223.
22. For more on the work of Thomas Lewis Seaman, see Trask, *Life How Short*, p. 73.
23. Cumberland County Deeds (PANS RG 47) Book I, p. 86.
24. C.J. Stewart "Brick Investigation Prescott House Nova Scotia" Historic Materials Research, Restoration Services Division, Parks Canada, Department of Indian and Northern Affairs, n.d., c.1974, unpublished report.
25. McNabb, "Land and Families in Horton Township" chapter 3.
26. Harley J. McKee, "Early Ways of Quarrying and Working Stone in the United States", *Bulletin of the Association for Preservation Technology* III no. I (1971) p. 44-58.
27. The vast majority of Seaman's stones are located in Kings County, in the area of the old Horton and Cornwallis townships. A few can be found around the old townships of Amherst, Granville, Londonderry and Halifax, although none of his stones is in the Newport or Falmouth township areas. Nor are there any gravestones in his style of carving found in all of north Cumberland, except for two in the present village of River Philip.

Fig. 1. Ryerson Tomb, complete view
(All photographs are by the author.)

POEMS IN STONE: THE TOMBS OF LOUIS HENRI SULLIVAN

Robert A. Wright

Introduction

Louis Henri Sullivan, generally acknowledged as the "Father of American Architecture," holds a unique position in nineteenth-century architectural history. Balancing organic and functional principles, he created buildings of unforgettable originality. Any artist is the product of his or her own time, either by contributing to current trends or ideas, or by reacting against them and starting out in new directions. Although Sullivan worked within the tradition of nineteenth-century Romanticism, he vehemently rejected much of the architecture of his era because it imitated past styles. Yet he studied historical styles in order to create an architectural vocabulary that revealed the psyche of his own times.

Sullivan devoted his life work to the development of an all-encompassing personal philosophy, which he expressed through both literary and architectural means. Although he remained a serious and prolific writer throughout his life, he conveyed his ideas more clearly through the grammar of architecture. For Sullivan, architecture

> is but the condensed expression of such philosophy as is held by the worker who creates it. It stands for his views... of Nature, of Man as an entity in nature, of his fellow men, of an infinite pervading and guiding Spirit... in short, his philosophy of life.[1]

Many scholars consider Sullivan's tombs as landmarks of his artistic evolution. The tombs remain in fine condition (in contrast to the fate of many of his buildings) as splendid embodiments of his spirit. Mausoleum commissions provided Sullivan with the opportunity to test his design skills and architectural principles on pure forms. As utilitarian functions were minimal, he could concentrate on the issues of his artistic development. Designing tombs allowed him to express his transcendentalist philosophy on an intimate architectural level. As the architectural historian Garcia-Menocal has noted,

> A work of architecture, to Sullivan, was a living entity. In the realm of the symbolic, a tomb becomes much more than a mere place of burial; it is a metaphor describing the economy pervading the universe... There is a vibrant and full life, that of the building, sustained by and existing because of death.[2]

An examination of the three tombs Sullivan designed provides a way to examine the development of his ideas within limited parameters. In order to do this successfully, one must first investigate his architectural and philosophical sources, as both were inextricably bound together. Only through a broad understanding of the influences behind his creativity can the significance of the tombs be understood and appreciated.

During the late nineteenth century, American architecture was at a pivotal juncture in its development. Many architects, in an effort to evoke the spirit of a style, carefully observed and followed the rules of past styles, including the exact copying of ornamental details. But a few American architects were developing a more innovative approach. Although they received their architectural education in Europe (or an equivalent European-style education in America), and depended on European source books, these architects used Western historical sources to evolve new forms.

Sullivan intuitively gravitated toward those architects who advanced a new style of American architecture. Frank Furness, the youthful Sullivan's employer in Philadelphia, produced buildings "out of his head," and this approach was similar to Sullivan's. Furness developed an original, stylized ornamentation derived from the Gothic Revival, and this was an important influence on Sullivan's botanically-based ornament.[3]

Sullivan's first employer in Chicago, William LeBaron Jenney, emphasized the structural aspects of buildings. Jenney's method integrated other sources besides modern engineering, and he provided a valuable example for Sullivan, "by preaching functionalism, embracing romanticism, and damning mindless eclecticism."[4]

America's pre-eminent architect, Henry Hobson Richardson, also influenced Sullivan, who witnessed the building of Richardson's Brattle Street Church in Boston, and acknowledged the bold Romanesque Revival masterpiece as a source of inspiration. Later, the monumental forcefulness and simplified form of Richardson's Marshall Field Wholesale Store in Chicago provided a bold statement for Sullivan to study.⁵

Leopold Eidlitz, who had collaborated with Richardson on the design of the state capitol building at Albany, was a distinguished New York architect who also impressed Sullivan. However, it was not Eidlitz's architectural style which attracted Sullivan, but his book, *The Nature and Function of Art, More Especially of Architecture*. Eidlitz contended that the purpose of studying architectural history lay not in the imitation of actual forms, but in learning their principles, for

> ...a monument, like any other work of art, is the expression of an idea in matter, and that to create a monument, the first step is to apprehend its idea... the styles of the past would doubtless furnish valuable examples of given problems solved, to the end that other problems may be solved upon the same principles...⁶

Eidlitz's theory of organic forms particularly influenced Sullivan. Studying nature and using historical sources served similar purposes for Eidlitz; both were a means to understand design solutions.

> The creations of art are subject to the same laws as those of nature... Natural organisms serve the purpose of teaching the relation of form to function... Art shall be directed to the creation of an organism which, like the organic productions of nature, performs a function...⁷

Sullivan was well acquainted with the writings of Viollet-le-Duc. Although Viollet-le-Duc was a French architect of some note, it was chiefly his widely influential writings which were important to Sullivan, particularly *Discourses on Architecture*.⁸ Viollet-le-Duc advocated the use of new materials and techniques, stressing a union between engineering and architecture. His rationalistic views emphasized that structural elements should determine the style of a building.

Architects of the late nineteenth century were deeply involved in developing a philosophical basis for their work. A brief survey of Sullivan's philosophical sources will elucidate his ideas about architecture, and why sepulchral architecture was especially appropriate to convey these intentions. He developed a comprehensive system of belief which encompassed aesthetics, theology, and sociology. Sullivan's intellectual pursuits were wide-ranging; he drew upon numerous nineteenth-century literary and philosophical sources.

He praised the positivism of the English philosopher Herbert Spencer, found in "Synthetic Philosophy" and *First Principles of a New System of Philosophy*.[9] The writings of Friedrich Nietzsche also captured Sullivan's attention; both men shared an ardent appreciation of the expressive power of Wagner's music, highly valuing such monumental examples of individual human creativity. Sullivan owned a copy of the first English translation of Nietzsche's *Thus Spoke Zarathustra*.[10] Another German, Friedrich Froebel, influenced Sullivan's thoughts concerning education. Froebel originated the kindergarten system, stressing the perception of nature as an instructional means to become conscious of God. The title and contents of Sullivan's *Kindergarten Chats*, reflected his familiarity with Froebel's book *The Education of Man*.[11] The writings of the French philosopher, literary critic, and art historian, Hippolyte Taine, also contributed to Sullivan's conceptual outlook. He was a professor at the Ecole des Beaux Arts where Sullivan attended the architecture program. Taine's essays, "The Philosophy of Art" and "The Ideal in Art," published in *Lectures on Art*, stressed the close relationship between society and art, and the conviction that a nation's culture would be reflected in its art.[12]

It remained for two indigenous American writers, however, to complete Sullivan's philosophical quest, and to place transcendentalist ideas firmly at the center of his philosophical system. Ralph Waldo Emerson's *Nature* and *Thoughts on Art*, published in the first half of the nineteenth century, securely established transcendentalism in America.[13] Subsequently, Walt Whitman's *Leaves of Grass* confirmed Sullivan's own search for a way to express America's national values.

Whitman's poetic lyricism struck a responsive chord in Sullivan, and his writings were abundantly indebted to Whitman. Sullivan's essay "Inspiration," which contained his fundamental beliefs, was written in the form of a prose poem and reflected many of Whitman's themes. Sullivan sent Whitman a devotional letter with a copy of "Inspiration." In this letter Sullivan stated,

> To a Man who can resolve himself into subtle unison with Nature and Humanity as you have done, who can blend the soul harmoniously with materials, who sees good in all and overflows in sympathy toward all things, enfolding them with his spirit: to such a man I joyfully give the name of Poet--the most precious of all names.[14]

Sullivan's lofty praise of Whitman revealed his own aspiration to express poetically the American spirit.

The Rural Cemetery Movement

A central theme of Romanticism was communion with nature for spiritual enrichment. This concept not only comprised the core of Sullivan's philosophy, but was also a founding precept of the rural cemetery movement.[15] Rural cemeteries and Sullivan's architecture therefore shared a mutual purpose. The task of designing mausolea for man-made landscapes which were created in accord with his own ideas was thus extraordinarily suitable for Sullivan. Jobs which involved sharing such a close common premise were rare, and this explains the lavish attention he spent on the small commissions.[16]

Sullivan reached an appreciation of nature at an early age through many family outings in the countryside surrounding Boston. On these excursions, in which his mother skillfully sketched plants, Sullivan was exposed to botanical drawing. Another early influence, Moses Woolson, was Sullivan's teacher at Boston English High School. Woolson used *Gray's School and Field Book of Botany* to teach studies on plants. The author, Professor Asa Gray of Harvard, even occasionally came to the school to speak on botany. The introduction of structural botany was of primary importance to Sullivan's development of architectural ornament. His ideas and writings used the model of organic growth.

One vivid early childhood experience particularly illustrates Sullivan's attraction to nature. Louis was left to his grandparents' care in 1868, when his parents moved to Chicago in hopes of improving his mother's health. But the next year his grandmother died. He was greatly moved by his first encounter with death and its accompanying sense of loss. As was the custom, the funeral service took place at home and was an intensely felt family experience. Yet the solemn and mournful affair was in contradiction to his feelings, and he sought comfort outdoors:

> ...a peach tree in full bloom in the garden caught his eye. He hastened to it as a friend, in dire need. Its joyous presence in the garden gave him courage, for spring again was singing her great song. The air was vocal of resurrection and life. Here indeed was resurrection and the life... Thus near the peach tree in full bloom Louis's tortured mind was stilled. He accepted death as evanishment, he accepted life as the power of powers.[17]

Sullivan's early feelings concerning death correspond to the ideals of the rural cemetery movement.[18] The aesthetics of a picturesque landscape relieved grief and nourished positive feelings. Nature provided a quiet inspirational setting for communion with God and fostered the theme of reunion with the souls of the deceased.

Sullivan embraced the progression of seasons as the primary allegory pertaining to the cycles of life and death. He employed a poetic writing style to portray the changing seasons, using a musical analogy to rephrase the seasonal rhythms of nature. Nature became a symphony, its movements the seasons.

In his symbolic essay "Inspiration," he wrote:

GROWTH - A SPRING SONG
O, soft, melodious springtime! First-born of life and love!
DECADENCE - AUTUMN REVERIE
...a great life has passed into the tomb, and there awaits the requiem of winter's snows.[19]

Sullivan elaborated on this theme of regeneration in his unpublished manuscript called *Natural Thinking*. The section entitled "Man and the Infinite" declared:

> ...it is change that makes us conscious of Life and the Flow of Life...a flow so constant in its double aspect that we call one manifestation of it Growth, and its corollary Death. These various considerations lead us to look on Life as...an essence so vast, so compelling, so completely integral, that death disappears; individual Life vanishes; and there remains...The sense of an Infinite that is Complete...It is to this Infinite that all Nature harkens.[20]

The same lessons of natural theology were advocated by observers of Mount Auburn, in Cambridge near Boston, the nation's first rural cemetery. They did not view death as final, for "in the mighty system of the universe, not a single step of the destroyer, Time, is made subservient to some ulterior purpose of reproduction, and the circle of creation and destruction is eternal." Mount Auburn established that "a rural cemetery is a school of both religion and philosophy" and set the precedent for rural cemeteries to pursue the moral education of the public.[21] Architecture for Sullivan served similar didactic purposes.

In essence rural cemeteries were founded for the very reasons Sullivan valued natural settings. The lessons of nature became crucial to his architectural and intellectual thought. All three of his mausolea express the ideals of the rural cemetery movement, and in fact were erected in prominent Midwestern rural cemeteries.[22]

Ryerson Tomb

Sullivan received his first mausoleum commission in 1887 at the age of thirty. It was for Martin Ryerson, a wealthy Chicago businessman whose fortune, derived from the building boom in Chicago, was made through the sale of lumber, real estate, and later, steel. The firm Adler and Sullivan had designed four office buildings for Ryerson prior to his death.

The most notable feature of the Ryerson Tomb is its massive solidity (Fig.1). Sullivan counteracted its formidable bulk and imposing appearance by employing two methods. First, the huge blocks of blue-black Quincy granite were highly polished to reflect the landscape. This enables the mausoleum to join its surroundings harmoniously and visually reinforced Sullivan's transcendentalist ideas. Second, the tomb's sloping walls and upward thrusting shape create an ascending form which again suggests regeneration.

The Ryerson Tomb shows how quickly Sullivan had absorbed the lessons from H. H. Richardson's buildings and had adapted them into an architectural grammar entirely his own. Like Richardson, Sullivan used massive forms to create a masculine edifice of monumental simplicity. But Sullivan eliminated Richardson's rustic ashlar walls and replaced them with polished granite, emphasizing the surface (as opposed to Richardson's emphasis on mass). The severity of mass and surface in the Ryerson Tomb marks the extreme of Sullivan's simplification.

In addition to absorbing influences from Richardson, Sullivan was seeking to learn the function of ornament, as he wrote:

> I take it as self-evident that a building, quite devoid of ornament, may convey a noble and dignified sentiment by virtue of mass and proportion...it would be greatly for our aesthetic good if we should refrain entirely from the use of ornament for a period of years, in order that our thought might concentrate acutely upon the production of buildings well formed and comely in the nude...This step taken, we might safely inquire to what extent a decorative application of ornament would enhance the beauty of our structures -- what new charm it would give them.[23]

Thus Sullivan's temporary avoidance of ornament was the result of a conscious effort. He realized this self-imposed limitation would benefit his subsequent use of ornament. However, Sullivan did not entirely eliminate ornament in the Ryerson Tomb. He designed a small grille for a high rear window, but it is a minor part of the whole effect. More importantly, a decorative lockplate, consisting of leaves represented in a naturalistic manner, adorns the bronze gate (Fig. 2). Sullivan had not yet developed his method for abstracting forms from nature. The leaves do not exhibit his mature ornamental style, although they convey the sense of fluid movement characteristic of Sullivan's botanically-derived ornament. The bronze leaves on the lockplate were an important antecedent to his mature work.[24]

Richardson was not the only influence on the tomb's design. The use of historical forms is evident. Egypt's ancient civilization provided Sullivan with appropriate prototypes for mortuary architecture. He combined the two sepulchral forms of a mastaba and pyramid.[25] The mastaba, a blocklike structure with sloping sides and a flat top, provided a base for the surmounting four-coursed pyramid. He used Egyptian massiveness in the Ryerson Tomb to create an impression of endurance and grandeur.

Contemporary sources of Egyptian-inspired architecture probably lured Sullivan to its use. Egyptian architecture had already been adopted for a variety of applications in rural cemeteries. Gateways, sphinxes, pyramids, and tombs with sloping sides had become an integral part of the American commemorative funerary tradition. Victorian era society strongly valued moralizing endeavors, and admired the respect for the dead displayed by Egypt's ancient civilization. Many of Egypt's finest buildings were enormous funerary structures that exuded a timeless aura. Because of these associations Egyptian architecture seemed especially appropriate for American cemeteries.[26]

The Monadnock Block of 1889-92 in downtown Chicago, designed by Sullivan's friend John Wellborn Root, is probably another reason that Sullivan decided to use Egyptian forms for the Ryerson Tomb. Root's Monadnock, the highest building supported by load-bearing masonry walls ever built, was the culmination of his life's work. The esteem in which Sullivan held Root and his work was noted in Sullivan's autobiography. Root died tragically, at the age of forty-one, before the building's completion, "leaving in Louis' heart and mind a deep sense of vacancy and loss...For John Root had it in him to be great..."[27]

Fig. 2. Ryerson Tomb, lockplate detail

Although the Monadnock (1889-92) was built after the Ryerson Tomb (1887), Root had completed a front elevation of the building in 1885, which clearly showed its swelling sides and other Egyptian motifs.[28] Since Sullivan and Root shared not only friendship but also close business and aesthetic interests, it is likely that Sullivan was aware of the interesting development of Root's Monadnock. The sparse use of ornament in the Monadnock, its simplified massive form, and its upward-thrusting visual movement all suggest Sullivan knew of Root's interest in the monumentality of Egyptian architecture.[29]

In addition to similarities of form, there is a remarkable similarity of intention between the Monadnock Block and the Ryerson Tomb. Root's Monadnock design was a visual metaphor for the commercial vitality of Chicago. Martin Ryerson, one of Chicago's most important businessmen, greatly contributed to the city's commercial development. Sullivan appropriately designed a mausoleum of commanding presence to represent Ryerson's achievements.

The arresting forcefulness of the Ryerson Tomb also results from Sullivan's doctrine of "Form Follows Function." However, this tenet of his architectural theory has often been misinterpreted because of a mechanistic twentieth-century bias.[30] Although Sullivan did emphasize the importance of utility, "the conception of functionalism, as set forth by Sullivan... calls for emotional and spiritual realities as well as physical realities."[31]

Sullivan felt that design solutions were to be found in the "essence of every problem." The "problem" of the Ryerson Tomb design was to express the quality of monumentality. Sullivan believed that

> there should be a function, a purpose, a reason for each building, a definite explainable relation between the form, and the causes that bring it into that particular shape; and that the building, to be good architecture, must, first of all, clearly correspond with its function, must be its image.[32]

Getty Tomb

Henry Harrison Getty was a business partner of Martin Ryerson and was familiar with Sullivan's work for Ryerson. When Getty's wife died in 1890, he hired Sullivan to design a family mausoleum. The Getty Tomb is remarkably different from the Ryerson Tomb, because Sullivan's style had evolved considerably during the passing of three busy years of design work. In recognition of the significance of the tomb, it was designated a Chicago Landmark in 1971 (Fig. 3). The commemorative plaque in front of the tomb states:

> The Getty Tomb marks the maturity of Sullivan's architectural style and the beginning of modern architecture in America. Here the architect departed from historic precedent to create a building of strong geometric massing, detailed with original ornament.

Sullivan's organic theory provided the basis for the Getty Tomb's creation. To fully understand Sullivan's ideas concerning its design, two central questions must be addressed. First, what motivated Sullivan's creative impulse? And second, how did his creative production take place? The answers lie in his belief that man was a spiritual being. Sullivan wrote:

> ... the most profound desire that fills the human soul... is the wish to be at peace with Nature and the Inscrutable Spirit... the greatest Art Work is that which most nearly typifies a realization of this... final peace: the peace of perfect equilibrium, the repose of absolute unity, the serenity of complete identification.[33]

In short, the creation of the Getty Tomb was a spiritual endeavor.

Sullivan outlined a trilogy of components necessary for creative production to occur: Imagination, Thought, and Expression. The sequence began with Imagination because this contained a vital dormant potential. For Sullivan "Man's Powers" unlocked the potential which brought forth the latent entity into being. In this way, Sullivan created the Getty Tomb out of its inorganic form. He purposefully chose its block-form to symbolize the inert matter which was "brought to 'life' by the 'power' of human imagination."[34] As Sullivan explained,

Fig. 3. Getty Tomb, complete view

> ...[by] the word inorganic is commonly understood that which is lifeless, or appears to be so; as stone... But nothing is really inorganic to the creative will of man. His spiritual power masters the inorganic and causes it to live in forms which his imagination brings forth from the lifeless...[35]

The block-form of the Getty Tomb is an excellent example of Sullivan's buildings which used that shape. Throughout his career, the block served as the basis for further elaboration. His repeated attraction to the block-form was attributable to his belief that it represented the aesthetic and symbolic qualities of the male nude form. Sullivan's admiration of the male physique led to his concept of heroic masculinity. The childhood experience of swimming naked with his father provided an early event to evoke the image "of a company of naked mighty men, with power to do splendid things with their bodies."[36] He glorified athletic abilities and the physical accomplishments of men. For Sullivan, "MAN THE WORKER becomes MAN THE CREATOR."

Sullivan's appreciation of the male form was later rekindled upon his discovery of Michelangelo's work. The nudes of the Sistine Chapel frescoes awed Sullivan when he viewed them as an architecture student. He felt the power of creativity and the heroic feats it could achieve. Sullivan sought to make the creative power expressed in Michelangelo's art the basis for his architecture.[37]

An equally powerful inspiration was provided by Richardson's newly completed Marshall Field Wholesale Store in Chicago. The simplified form of the massive edifice ended Sullivan's search for a masculine architectural icon. Many of his buildings, including the Getty Tomb, owe their block-form to Richardson's "manly" and "virile" expression of "procreant power" (Sullivan's terms). Like Michelangelo, Richardson provided Sullivan with a means to express formally the first step in creative process: Imagination.

The next component of Sullivan's system, Thought, provided an orderly method for working with the physical materials and provided a logical means for constructing the tomb. For Sullivan, thought was a rational process, and consequently was responsible for all engineering aspects. Therefore, the components of the Getty Tomb were assembled according to rational building principles.

The tomb is placed on a stylobate (base-block) which provides a firm foundation to support its weight and to balance visually the large cornice. This cornice is one indication of the precision used to integrate the individual structural components. Rather than being added, the cornice is created by an extension of the roof members. The roof is constructed of three large stone slabs, each gracefully curving upward. In addition to adding visual delight, the curved slabs channel water away from the masonry joints. This is an example of a rational, as opposed to a symbolic, application of Sullivan's axiom that "Form Follows Function."

Sullivan believed that the arch was not only a structural device, but, more important, embodied the creative power of man. Sullivan created arched openings for the tomb's door (Fig. 3) and two opposing side windows. The arches pierce the mass of the block, prompting a spatial dynamism. The arch represented for Sullivan the pinnacle of architectural thought; as he eloquently stated:

> It is difficult to conceive the arch as a creation of a single mind; I do not recall an instance of creative power approaching this in grandeur. To the reflective mind the arch is a wonder, a marvel, a miracle."[38]

Expression, the last component of Sullivan's system, provided a contrasting function to Thought by supplying the lyrical sensibilities necessary for the "perfection of the physical" structure. The choice of material and ornamental design was a means to express emotions, for Sullivan, a feminine characteristic. Especially because the Getty Tomb was to memorialize a woman, it was fashioned in a delicate manner. The tomb is constructed of pale Bedford limestone, a stone Sullivan selected for its characteristic transparent shadows. This soft lighting effect creates a sense of buoyancy. The finely-carved ornamental pattern of the upper half of the exterior walls also lightens visually the mass of the tomb. The tomb's ornament was Sullivan's vehicle for beautification.

Since communing with Nature was essential for Sullivan's creative process, many of the tomb's ornamental designs stem from organic forms. Through studying the growth of these organic forms, Sullivan claimed that the "Flow of Life" could be perceived. This "rhythm" was the principle of creation used by the "Infinite Creative Spirit." Nature's system of production, once understood, could then be emulated by man. Using this principle, Sullivan created several original motifs inspired by organic models. The beaded "stars" of the Getty Tomb are representative of growth patterns which are found in many sea invertebrates such as starfish. Further evidence of Sullivan's use of biological forms can be found in the band of spiral-scroll ornament of the cornice. Cellular divisions within the scrolls bear a close resemblance to certain sea shells, such as the chambered nautilus (Fig. 4).

The vegetal motifs of the Getty Tomb resulted from Sullivan's ardent interest in plant forms. His attraction to the principles of vegetative growth was an effort to understand "the universal power or energy which flows everywhere at all times, in all places, seeking expression in form, and thus parallel to all things."[39] He used Gray's *Botany* and Edmund B. Wilson's *The Cell in Development and Inheritance* to learn about plant morphology and biological growth.

Fig. 4. Getty Tomb, cornice ornament detail

Through his botanical studies, Sullivan learned about the cotyledons of young plants, and these provided another symbolic analogy for his philosophy. He believed the germ-seed, which contained the nutrients for growth, represented creative potential: "The Germ is the real thing; the seat of identity. Within its delicate mechanism lies the will to power: the function which is to seek and eventually find its full expression in form."[40]

Beyond providing Sullivan with a source for ornamental design, organic growth furnished him with the basis of symbolic power. Thus the power implicit in organic growth was for him the guide to the creation of his ornamental motifs. This was parallel to the manner in which the male nude provided symbolic power for the block form of the tomb.

In summary, the origin of the Getty Tomb depended on Sullivan's system of creative production. The trilogy of Imagination, Thought, and Expression furnished him with a method for designing his art. Exceptional examples of artistic expression, such as the works of Michelangelo and Richardson, inspired Sullivan to strive for a similar level of excellence. In a like manner, Sullivan examined historical sources which could provide solutions for design problems. The chief historical sources he turned to were Greek and Islamic design.

Art reference books supplied Sullivan with elements for elaborating his organic-design system. Two important source books influenced the development of Sullivan's botanical ornament: V.M.C. Ruprich-Robert's *Flore Ornementale* and Owen Jones's *The Grammar of Ornament*.[41] The significance of these sources lies in their common approach to historical styles.

Ruprich-Robert, a professor at the Ecole des Arts Décoratifs in Paris, was a leader of the Néo-Grec movement. He studied a method of abstracting decorative motifs from actual plant forms.[42] Owen Jones, the prominent English decorative designer, presented the world history of ornament in one monumental book. Its last chapter, "Leaves and Flowers from Nature," contained botanical drawings and his conclusion:

> ... in the best periods of art all ornament was rather based upon an observation of the principles which regulate the arrangement of form in nature, than on an attempt to imitate the absolute forms of those works... true art consisting in idealizing, and not copying, the forms of nature... [43]

Both Ruprich-Robert and Jones studied historical styles as a means to discover the artistic intentions of past civilizations.

Through Ruprich-Robert and Jones, Sullivan discovered the basis of Greek ornamental aesthetics which influenced his compositions of the Getty Tomb's vegetal motifs. The graceful foliage of the tomb's bronze gate (Figs. 5 and 6) and door reflects the Greek formulation of three principles of natural growth: "radiation from the parent stem, the proportionate distribution of areas, and the tangential curvature of the lines."[44]

The bead-and-reel motif of the door archivolt and the fretwork of the bronze gate hinge are examples of classical details which appeared throughout Sullivan's career. Both clearly show his conscious use of Greek ornament. According to the early architectural historian Montgomery Schuyler, Sullivan copied the bead-and-reel motif from H. H. Richardson's porch of Austin Hall at Harvard.[45]

In addition to classical designs, the rich ornament of the Getty Tomb contains other historical motifs. The tracery of the gate medallions is curiously Celtic in design. The interwoven spirals share both form and feeling with similar designs carved on Celtic cross memorials (Figs. 5 and 6).

Sullivan's desire to break away from the associations of western ornament led to his interest in Islamic sources. His search for an architecture of unity required the transcendence of western attitudes and traditions. The ubiquitous presence of Islamic ornament (and its endless variety) was contrary to western aesthetic thought. The hierarchical arrangement of ornamental elements to emphasize an architectural form was absent, indicating a fundamental difference in purpose. The eastern transcendental emphasis on the sublime replaced the western concern for the contemplation of beauty. According to Keith Critchlow, an expert on Islamic design, Islamic ornamental patterns were, "a means of relating multiplicity to Unity by means of mathematical forms which are seen, not as mental abstractions, but as reflections of the celestial archetypes within both the cosmos and the minds and souls of men."[46]

The Getty Tomb's octagonal pattern shares a number of common affinities with Islamic art and architecture. Although Sullivan did not replicate an existing pattern, diaper ornament was used exclusively in Islamic

Fig. 5. Getty Tomb, bronze gate detail

Fig. 6. Getty Tomb, second bronze gate detail

buildings to produce two dimensional patterns. This mosaic-like pattern gave a nonstatic emphasis to the surface. Sullivan applied this treatment to the exterior of the tomb's upper half, which accentuated the door and windows, thereby relieving the heaviness of the cubic mass (Figs. 7 and 8). His maintenance of the western emphasis on building openings gives the tomb a resemblance to certain Moorish-style mausolea erected in Morocco, where the western architectural tradition of featuring portals was assimilated into Islamic architecture.[47] The geometrical motifs allowed Sullivan to unite his artistic and architectural talents in the spirit of Islamic thought.

In the Getty Tomb, Sullivan employed architectural features of both western and eastern historical styles. Classical ornament influenced his botanical designs while Islamic antecedents supplied the inspiration for the geometrical patterns. The skillful intermingling of morphological and geometric ornament enabled Sullivan to achieve a vibrant ornamentation. Although he used some historical details, they chiefly supplemented his original designs.

Fig. 7. Getty Tomb, ornament detail from door archivolt

Fig. 8. Getty Tomb, side view

Many of Sullivan's writings discuss his ornamental theory, and affirm the significant role ornament performs in his architecture. Two years after the completion of the Getty Tomb a summation of his principles was published as "Ornament in Architecture."[48] This close chronological sequence suggests that designing this tomb helped Sullivan develop fully his ornamental theory. A brief summary of this essay by the historian of Sullivan's ornament, Paul Sprague, lists the following central ideas:

1. Ornament should seek to express a subjective quality.
2. Architectural ornament should form an integral, organic part of the entire architectural composition.
3. Ornament should appear to be of the surface, not on it.
4. The qualities of the ornament should be related to the qualities of the building as a whole.
5. All basic decisions about architectural ornament should be made when the initial design is prepared.[49]

Fig. 9. Getty Tomb, cornice ornament detail

Sullivan used traditional means to implement this theory of ornament. The Getty Tomb shows that his arrangement of individual motifs within a pattern, and the placement of these patterns on the tomb, were employed for conventional purposes: "to mark structural divisions, to emphasize architectural climaxes, and to moderate texturally the harshness of stone."[50]

Specific examples clearly illustrate each of these points. Both the bead-and-reel and vegetal motifs demarcate the voussoirs (wedge-shaped units of an arch) (Fig. 9). The outlining of the lower cornice edge is a further example of Sullivan's use of ornament to distinguish building component functions (Figs. 7 and 8). Two ornamental patterns serve to accent the arches: the concentric bands of the archivolts (Fig. 9) and the octagonal pattern of the upper walls. All of the tomb's ornament serves to modulate light to create textural interest. However, because the octagonal motif is the largest ornament design, and is used to create an extensive pattern, it most prominently exhibits that function (Fig. 10).

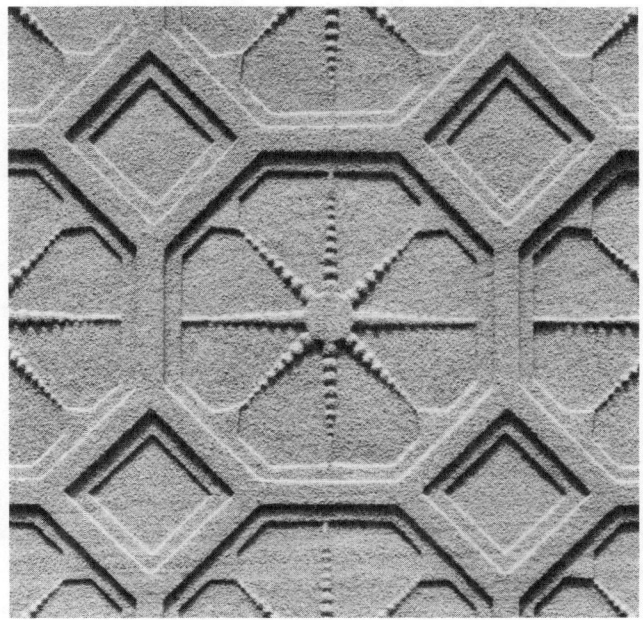

Fig. 10. Getty Tomb, octagonal ornament detail

The Getty Tomb was Sullivan's most successful building design in which ornament and mass are interdependent. Ornament was not used as decoration only, but played an important role in determining the actual building design. Sullivan calculated carefully the symmetry of the tomb, its proportions determined by the size of the octagonal motif. The number of octagons creates the 3:4 proportion in the plan of the tomb. The facade has twelve octagons to a row, while the sides contain sixteen per row (12:16 or 3:4). Two semicircular windows with decorative bronze grilles create lunettes which are exactly centered on the side walls (Fig. 11). The door is also precisely centered on the front wall. The window and door archivolts and their concentric ornamental banding correspond to nodes of the octagonal pattern. Furthermore, the dimensions of the voussoirs are also determined by the octagonal measurements.[51] (Figs. 7 and 8)

The complete integration of ornament and mass was a fundamental concern of Sullivan, for "the ornament should appear, not as something receiving the spirit of the structure, but as a thing expressing that spirit by virtue

Fig. 11. Getty Tomb, bronze window grille

of differential growth."[52] The physical method employed to carve the tomb's ornament strengthens this contention. Described as intaglio, the motifs were carved out of the stone, contrary to the usual method of relief carving which projects the ornament into space. Sullivan specifically wanted the ornament to lie below the stone's surface in order to unite it closely with the tomb's mass. With the Getty Tomb, Sullivan achieved his goals of unity and balance.

The ornament of the Getty Tomb is perfectly balanced, both within its internal organization and in its harmonious relationship to the tomb's structure. Emanuel Swedenborg, the eighteenth-century scientist, mystic, and religious philosopher, advanced a theory of "correspondences," which provided Sullivan with an ideological structure for ordering the themes that determined his architecture. Swedenborg believed that "the realms of the physical and spiritual were part of a transcendent totality," and that creation depended on the balance of opposing characteristics. Therefore, according to Swedenborg, "correspondences" existed between the polarized dualities of wisdom/love, reason/emotion, and masculine/feminine: the formative forces of the universe.[53]

Sullivan created correspondences of his own. The pairing of contrary design traits, such as mass/detail and geometric/organic, allowed Sullivan to establish a perfect compositional balance. The tomb's massive block-form was imbued with masculine rational qualities, while its contrasting ornament embodied feminine emotional attributes. Ornament itself was also designed according to this idea; vegetal motifs were feminine and lyrical, while the octagonal pattern was masculine and logical. The reconciliation of opposites was viewed by Sullivan as a creative principle conforming to the generative process of the universe.

The Getty Tomb manifests the culmination of Sullivan's search for an architecture of unity. His approach to architecture was predicated on a personal philosophy which interwove themes of theology, biology, aesthetics, and mathematics. Sullivan was eclectic, basing his philosophy on a variety of sources. Theories of masculine power, American transcendentalism, Greek and Islamic aesthetics, and the teachings of Emanuel Swedenborg all contributed to the theoretical infrastructure of his architecture. Sullivan's eclecticism was not indiscriminate, however. He purposefully sought out ideologies which presented ideas parallel to his own. Concepts from these various sources were combined into his unique vision, with the primary purpose to explain the creative forces of creation. Sullivan's first building to be designed via this guiding philosophy was the Getty Tomb. Its exquisite realization of aesthetic unity caused Frank Lloyd Wright to remark:

> The Getty Tomb in Graceland Cemetery was entirely his own; fine sculpture. A statue. A great poem addressed to human sensibilities as such. Outside the realm of music what finer requiem?[54]

Wainwright Tomb

The Wainwright Tomb commission resulted from Sullivan's professional travel. In St. Louis, Sullivan met Ellis Wainwright, a wealthy businessman, whose family fortune was made through brewing beer. Sullivan designed the renowned Wainwright Building (1890-91) for him. Its success pleased Wainwright. When his beautiful young wife died in 1891, Wainwright turned again to Sullivan. The resulting tomb, designed by Sullivan at the height of his creative powers, was another masterpiece (Fig. 12).

Fig. 12. Wainwright Tomb, complete view

Sullivan had integrated eastern and western traits in the Getty Tomb, but for Wainwright he abandoned western sources completely. The Wainwright Tomb was strongly imbued with Islamic design elements. Books on Islamic architecture in Sullivan's library attest to his interest. Islamic architects, designers, and calligraphers created forms based on the same natural forces they perceived to be responsible for the creation of all things in the universe. Islamic designs provided an alternative to western historical sources, and Sullivan embraced the spiritual unity of the Islamic world as means to create new forms.

The Wainwright Tomb is basically a domed cube, remarkably similar in form to a *qubba* a North African mausoleum. Three circular courses support the dome, its interior covered with a deep blue mosaic containing at the center a single golden star. The facade, with its elaborate ornamental friezes, is derivative of an Islamic *pistaq*, an imposing rectangular gateway (Fig. 13). Sullivan successfully integrated two Islamic architectural forms, the *qubba* and *pistaq*.[55]

An approach of three steps gives the Wainwright Tomb a sense of grandeur. On either side are blocklike forms serving both functional and aesthetic purposes. Sullivan designed the blocks large enough to create niches to accommodate benches. These exedras provide a place for visitors to rest and contemplate, in keeping with the concept of a mortuary monument. Sullivan employed these forms to broaden the composition of the tomb and unify and separate elements. They resemble cupulated structures called *chatris*, Islamic in origin, and often accompanying Indian mosque and tomb entrances.[56]

An examination of the tomb's ornamental friezes provides a means of assessing the degree to which Sullivan was indebted to Islamic designs. The curvilinear forms which accompany the vegetative motifs have lost all western likeness. They closely resemble the calligraphy found on Moslem buildings, yet Sullivan introduced new designs such as the large bulbous motifs he used in later designs.[57] The vegetal motifs of the Wainwright Tomb were reduced in size and importance from ornament designs of previous buildings. The extensive use of restraining geometrical designs indicated a shift in Sullivan's treatment of ornament toward an Islamic conception. The rear

Fig. 13. Wainwright Tomb, frontal view

frieze is primarily geometrical, with the spiky leaves tightly enclosed within intersecting circles (Fig. 14). In addition to its practical design application, Sullivan used the circle extensively for its symbolic connotations. In Islamic ornament, "the circle surpasses all other geometric patterns as the symbol of cosmic unity..."[58]

The "snowflake" frieze surrounding the door of the Wainwright Tomb is an excellent example of Sullivan's manipulation of geometric forms. Islamic artists used a technique in which new forms were created through geometrical subdivision. For example, the subdivision of a circle furnished a system for the creation of triangles, stars, hexagons, and other geometric shapes. The plates in Sullivan's *A System of Architectural Ornament* illustrate a similar use of the circle.[59]

Fig. 14. Wainwright Tomb, side view

The ornamental friezes provide the necessary vitality to enliven and unify the tomb's composition. Curvilinear motifs were used repetitiously to create an exuberant sense of motion within the confines of the frieze. The motifs, essential for balancing the massive static forms, symbolize universal regenerative qualities. Sullivan's efforts went far beyond the tomb's design requirements, however; he created a different ornamental motif for the frieze of each of the four tomb walls. These large friezes define the wall perimeters, while simultaneously accentuating the door and window openings (Fig. 15). Vegetal motifs predominate in the front and side friezes, containing spiky leaves and bulbous forms. One side frieze features pods (Fig. 16). Inside the pods are seeds, which played the central role in Sullivan's system of organic ornament. For him, seeds expressed the potential for the creation of forms. The seed pods are a visual representation of this theory; they were at the origin of the flowing vegetal forms of the ornamental frieze.

Fig. 15. Wainwright Tomb, ornament detail of side window

Fig. 16. Wainwright Tomb, ornament detail from side frieze

Fig. 17. Wainwright Tomb, ornament detail of rear frieze

Ornament was Sullivan's foremost means of plastic expression. The extent to which he articulated his ideas visually can be viewed in the tomb's window treatment (Fig. 17). Here geometry is victorious. Through repetition, integration, and subdivision, Sullivan achieved a notable design composition. The bronze window grille consists of four large ellipses. Within these are contained three octagons (a shape carried over from the Getty Tomb ornament). Further geometrical subdivision created ellipses within the interstices of the octagons, and finally four-pointed "stars" within those ellipses. The total composition reverberates between the constantly conflicting sensations of expansion and contraction. A decorative frieze was then employed to enclose the composition, using the same ellipse and "star" motifs found in the grille (Fig. 18). Via an Islamic design process, Sullivan had achieved total compositional unity.

Fig. 18. Wainwright Tomb, ornament detail from side window

With the greater assertiveness of geometrical motifs, Sullivan achieved in the Wainwright Tomb a new balance between geometric and organic forms. This equilibrium directly reflected the aesthetic and philosophical ideals of the Moslem world. Unity was achieved through the expression of polarities:

> Islamic art is predominantly a balance between pure geometrical form and what can be called fundamental biomorphic form: a polarization that has associative values with the four philosophical and experiential qualities of cold and dry - representing the crystallization in geometric form - and hot and moist - representing the formative forces behind vegetative and vascular form.[60]

Islamic thought provided another framework for the affirmation of Sullivan's transcendentalist philosophy.

Conclusion

The tombs of Louis Sullivan exemplify the ideas of a man living at the close of the nineteenth century. Sullivan formulated his Romantic philosophy from a variety of early personal experiences and literary sources. Indeed, Sullivan is within the tradition of Emerson, Thoreau, and Whitman.

Nineteenth-century America was trying to establish a cultural identity, yet people turned to the achievements of Western Europe for inspiration and models to imitate. Most American sepulchral buildings merely imitated past architectural styles. Those tombs dotted the rural cemetery landscape. Sullivan studied and derived useful information from historical example, but he used it for qualities that paralleled and strengthened his architectural theories. Sullivan's mausolea elevated American funerary architecture to a new stature.

His quest for understanding the creative forces of the universe led him to a transcendentalist philosophy. Although he assimilated the lessons of transcendentalism and appreciated the values of nature, Sullivan went far beyond traditional Romanticism. He also embraced a rational methodology, for technology and engineering were changing the face of the world. Sullivan's original architecture reflected his deeply-felt American sensibilities. Lewis Mumford summarizes his significance:

Sullivan was perhaps the first mind in American architecture that had come to know itself with any fullness in relation to its soil, its period, its civilization, and had been able to absorb fully all the many lessons of the century.[61]

Sullivan's three tombs were important milestones in his development as an architect. Minimizing the complex considerations of utilitarian use, he was able to focus his attention completely on pure aesthetics.[62] Because his philosophy was based on the cyclical progressions of nature, his designing of mausolea was especially appropriate. For Sullivan organic architecture was symbolic of the forces in the universe, and indicated the creative powers of man. He turned to Islamic architecture because it provided an alternative to historical western sources. The eastern belief that forms were created by oppositional forces paralleled his own views and provided a conceptual foundation for his search in achieving design unity. The three tomb commissions enabled Sullivan to represent his spiritual quest in physical form.

Postscript

Sullivan died in Chicago in 1924, a neglected and impoverished man. Thomas Tallmadge, the noted architectural historian, planned Sullivan's memorial, and financed it through private contributions. Standing near the Ryerson Tomb, in Chicago's Graceland Cemetery, the monument is a rough-hewn granite gravestone on which a bronze plaque is mounted (Fig. 19). The plaque is a replica of a Sullivan ornament drawing, #19 from his *System of Architectural Ornament*, surrounding a profile of Sullivan executed by C.P. Seidel (Fig. 20). Tallmadge wrote the epitaph which was carved on the back of the memorial.

Fig. 19. Sullivan gravestone, complete view

Fig. 20. Sullivan gravestone, bronze detail

1856   LOUIS HENRI SULLIVAN   1924
BY HIS BUILDINGS GREAT INFLUENCE AND POWER; HIS DRAWINGS
UNSURPASSED IN ORIGINALITY AND BEAUTY; HIS WRITINGS RICH IN
POETRY AND PROPHESY; HIS TEACHINGS PERSUASIVE AND ELOQUENT;
HIS PHILOSOPHY WHERE, IN "FORM FOLLOWS FUNCTION,"
HE SUMMED UP ALL TRUTH IN ART. SULLIVAN HAS EARNED HIS PLACE AS
ONE OF THE GREATEST ARCHITECTURAL FORCES IN AMERICA. IN
TESTIMONY OF THIS, HIS PROFESSIONAL AND OTHER FRIENDS HAVE
BUILT THIS MONUMENT.

The year before his death Sullivan had written:

> The architect who combines in his being the powers of vision, of imagination, of intellect, of sympathy with human need and the power to interpret them in a language vernacular and true - is he who shall create poems in stone... [63]

Appendix: A Catalogue Raisonne of Sullivan's Tombs[64]

RYERSON TOMB:

Location: Graceland Cemetery, Chicago, Illinois.
Commission: Martin A. Ryerson for his father Martin Ryerson who died September 6, 1887
Designed: September, 1887
Ornament: October, 1887
Source: Building Budget (Chicago, Illinois), November 30, 1887: "Lets Contracts"

GETTY TOMB:

Location: Graceland Cemetery, Chicago, Illinois
Commission: Henry H. Getty for Carrie Eliza Getty who died February 24, 1890
Designed: September, 1890
Ornament: October, 1890
Location of
Drawings: Avery Architectural Library, Columbia University, Frank Lloyd Wright Collection

WAINWRIGHT TOMB:

Location: Bellefontaine Cemetery, St. Louis, Missouri
Commission: Ellis Wainwright for Charlotte Dickson Wainwright who died April 15, 1891
Designed: November, 1891
Ornament: January, 1892
Location of
Drawings: University of Michigan, College of Architecture and Design. Working drawing is at Burnham Architectural Library, Chicago Art Institute. Perspective drawing published in "Inland Architect and News Record," XIX, May 1892.

NOTES

The author would like to thank Narciso G. Menocal for helpful suggestions upon reading the first draft of this article. Further thanks are due to Harold Allen and my brother, David C. Wright, for their careful editing of the article's final draft.

1. Louis Sullivan, *Kindergarten Chats and Other Writings*, (New York: Dover, 1979), 160. This is a reprint of the 1947 edition which contained Sullivan's revised manuscript of 1918, along with other essays by Sullivan.
2. Narciso Garcia-Menocal, "Louis Sullivan: His Theory, Mature Development, and Theme" (unpublished doctoral thesis, University of Illinois, Champaign-Urbana, 1974), 69.
3. Several writings explain Sullivan's indebtedness to Furness. See Paul E. Sprague, "The Architectural Ornament of Louis Sullivan and his Chief Draftsmen" (unpublished doctoral thesis, Princeton University, 1969). Refer to Part One, Section two: "The Origins of Louis Sullivan's Architectural Ornament, the Gothic Revival." For a more detailed examination of Furness, see James F. O'Gorman, *The Architecture of Frank Furness* (Philadelphia: Philadelphia Museum of Art, 1973).
4. Theodor Turak, as cited in Robert Twombly, *Louis Sullivan: His Life and Work* (New York: Viking, 1986), 53. For a thorough treatment of Jenney's architectural theory see Theodor Turak, *William LeBaron Jenney: A Pioneer of Modern Architecture* (Ann Arbor: UMI Research Press, 1986).
5. Sullivan's comments on Richardson's Brattle Street Church are in Louis Sullivan, *The Autobiography of an Idea* (New York: Dover, 1956, a reprint of the 1924 first edition), 188. Sullivan's impression of Richardson's Marshall Field Store appears in *Kindergarten Chats*, 30.
6. Leopold Eidlitz as cited in Menocal, "Louis Sullivan," 130.
7. *Ibid.*, 127 & 130.
8. The 1875 English translation of *Discourses on Architecture* and other books by Viollet-le-Duc were owned by Sullivan. A list of the books in Sullivan's personal library is included in the 1909 auction catalog for the sale of his possessions, located in the Burnham Library of the Art Institute of Chicago. A number of books touch upon the importance of Viollet-le-Duc to Sullivan. The most comprehensive discussion of these ideas is in Narciso G. Menocal, *Architecture as Nature: The Transcendentalist Idea of Louis Sullivan* (Madison: University of Wisconsin Press, 1981). In addition to noting the intellectual antecedents Viollet-le-Duc provided for Sullivan, Menocal observes similarities in their ornament as well. See the section entitled "Geometry & Ornamentation: Theory & Practice."

9. Evidence of Sullivan's affinity to Spencer's writings are in Frank Lloyd Wright, *Autobiography* (New York: Duell, Sloan & Pearce, 1943, a reprint of the 1932 first edition), 70. Twombly, 145 provides a condensed version of an 1882 interview with Sullivan.
10. Menocal, "Louis Sullivan," 157.
11. *Ibid.*, 121-124.
12. Menocal, *Architecture as Nature*, 11-12.
13. *Ibid.*, 44, 146, 192.
14. Cited in Sherman Paul, *Louis Sullivan: An Architect in American Thought* (Englewood Cliffs: Prentice-Hall, 1962), 2.
15. A growing number of books concerning America's cultural history treat the rural cemetery movement. An especially good analysis of the Romantic ideals responsible for the founding of rural cemeteries is found in James J. Farrell, *Inventing the American Way of Death, 1830-1920* (Philadelphia: Temple University Press, 1980), 30-34, 102-108.
16. During the five-year period in which the three tombs were built (1887-1892), the firm of Adler & Sullivan designed approximately thirty buildings. After the completion of Chicago's nationally acclaimed Auditorium in 1889, a plethora of commissions followed. The Getty Tomb (1890) was designed during the busiest time of Sullivan's career.
17. Sullivan, *Autobiography*, 171.
18. Among the primary causes for the establishment of rural cemeteries was the attitude that a natural landscape would provide solace to people suffering from melancholy. See David Schuyler, *The New Urban Landscape: The Redefinition of City Form in Nineteenth-Century America* (Baltimore: John Hopkins University Press, 1986), 40-41.
19. "Inspiration," reprinted in Menocal, *Architecture as Nature*, 156-167.
20. Reprinted in Maurice English, *The Testament of Stone: Themes of Idealism and Indignation from the Writings of Louis Sullivan* (Evanston: Northwestern University Press, 1963), 111.
21. Stanley French, "The Cemetery as Cultural Institution: The Establishment of Mount Auburn and the Rural Cemetery Movement" in *Death in America*, ed. David E. Stannard (University of Pennsylvania Press, 1975), 78-79.
22. The tombs of Ryerson and Getty are both located in Chicago's Graceland Cemetery. Sullivan undoubtedly was well aware of William LeBaron Jenney's landscape planning for Graceland, during his employment with Jenney. In fact the Getty Tomb was built facing Willowmere, the artificial lake Jenney had designed according to the ideals of Romantic landscape design. This orientation yields a charming reflection of the tomb in the still waters of Willowmere, showing that Sullivan was aware of picturesque landscape principles. For an account of Jenney's role in the design of Graceland's landscape, see Walter L. Creese, *The Crowning of the American Landscape* (Princeton: Princeton University Press, 1985), 208, 210-211.
23. Sullivan, "Ornament in Architecture" as reprinted in *Kindergarten Chats*, 187.
24. For a thorough treatment of the Ryerson Tomb lockplate design and its significance, see Sprague, 115, 123.
25. Barbara Lanctot, *A Walk Through Graceland Cemetery, revised edition* (Chicago: Chicago Architecture Foundation, 1982), 20.
26. The following sources include information and analysis pertaining to Egyptian Revival architecture in nineteenth-century rural cemeteries: Harold Allen, "Egypt (American Style): Photographs of Egyptian-style American Architecture" (unpublished exhibition catalog, Syracuse University, 1984); Richard G. Carrott, *The Egyptian Revival: Its Sources, Monuments, and Meanings: 1808-1858* (Berkeley, University of California Press, 1978); and James Stevens Curl, *The Egyptian Revival* (London: George Allen & Unwin, 1982).
27. Sullivan, *Autobiography*, 292.
28. Donald Hoffman, *The Architecture of John Wellborn Root* (Baltimore: John Hopkins University Press, 1973), 169.

29. At the request of his client, who wished to lessen building costs, Root designed a final plan which almost completely eliminated exterior ornament. However, Sullivan probably had no similar cost constraints for the Ryerson Tomb because of the family's immense wealth. Two buildings Sullivan had designed previously for Ryerson used Egyptian ornamental motifs on the facades. This indicates that Sullivan, like Root, was also interested in Egyptian architecture for aesthetic reasons.
30. The distinction between mechanistic and vitalistic sensibilities is developed by Sprague, 5-11.
31. Hugh Morrison, *Louis Sullivan: Prophet of Modern Architecture* (New York: W.W. Norton, 1935), 279.
32. Sullivan, *Kindergarten Chats*, 46.
33. *Ibid.*, 195.
34. William H. Jordy, *American Buildings and Their Architects: Volume Four, Progressive and Academic Ideals at the Turn of the Twentieth Century* (Oxford and New York: Oxford University Press, 1972), 105.
35. Louis Sullivan, *A System of Architectural Ornament According With a Philosophy of Man's Powers* (New York: Eakins Press, 1967, a reprint of the 1924 first edition), no page numbers, see the section, "The Inorganic and the Organic."
36. Sullivan, *Autobiography*, 79.
37. Menocal, "Louis Sullivan," 245-246.
38. Sullivan, *Kindergarten Chats*, 123.
39. Sullivan, *A System of Architectural Ornament*, see the section entitled "Interlude, the Doctrine of Parallelism."
40. *Ibid.*, see the section, "Prelude."
41. These major reference books were used internationally by architects for developing ornament designs. Sullivan became familiar with the books through both his architectural education and his employers.
42. The influence of the Néo-Grec Movement on Sullivan is described by David Van Zanten, "Sullivan to 1890," in *Louis Sullivan: The Function of Ornament* ed. Wim De Wit, (New York: W.W. Norton, 1986).
43. Owen Jones, *The Grammar of Ornament* (New York: Van Nostrand Reinhold, 1982, a reprint of the 1856 first edition), 154.
44. *History of Architecture and Ornament* (Scranton: International Textbook, 1928), 69. A full-size cast of the richly ornamented bronze door was made and sent to the Musée des Arts Décoratifs in Paris during 1893, and is now stored in the basement of the Louvre in Paris. Critical acclaim followed Sullivan's Paris exhibition and many casts were subsequently made for various European institutions. The Getty Tomb door and its award at the Paris Exposition of 1900 demonstrated European appreciation of Sullivan's ornament.
45. Montgomery Schuyler, "Architecture in Chicago: Adler & Sullivan," in *American Architecture and Other Writings*, ed. William H. Jordy and Ralph Coe, vol. 2, (Cambridge, Mass.: Harvard University Press, 1961), 401.
46. Keith Critchlow, *Islamic Patterns: An Analytical and Cosmological Approach* (London: Thames & Hudson, 1978), 6.
47. Menocal, *Architecture as Nature*, 34, 36.
48. Sullivan, *Kindergarten Chats*, 187-190. First published in "The Engineering Magazine," vol. 32, no. 5 (August 1892).
49. Sprague, 41-42.
50. *Ibid.*, 164.
51. A detailed description based on actual measurements is provided in Menocal, "Louis Sullivan," 66-68. Also see Menocal, *Architecture as Nature*, 35, for the author's diagram of the ornamentation.

52. Sullivan, *Kindergarten Chats*, 189.
53. Menocal, *Architecture as Nature*, 24-25.
54. Frank Lloyd Wright, *Genius and the Mobocracy* (New York: Horizon Press, 1971, a reprint of the 1949 first edition), 95.
55. Menocal, *Architecture as Nature*, 36, 40-42.
56. Menocal, "Louis Sullivan," 71-72.
57. Sprague, 184.
59. Critchlow, 58.
58. Although a number of plates illustrate Sullivan's use of the circle, plate #3 is a particularly good example.
60. *Ibid.*, 8.
61. Lewis Mumford, *The Brown Decades: A study of the Arts in America* (New York: Dover, 1955, a reprint of the 1931 first edition), 143.
62. Sullivan wanted the tombs to express perfectly his design ideas. Contrary to normal mausolea commissions, the Wainwright and Getty names were excluded from their tombs, as Sullivan wanted the facade compositions to be flawless. Sullivan had incorporated H.H. Getty's initials in the bronze window grilles, but apparently this identifying feature was not sufficient for Getty. The Getty name was subsequently carved into the voussoirs of the door arch. Early photographs depicting the Getty Tomb before the addition of its lettering show the superiority of Sullivan's original treatment. See Thomas E. Tallmadge, *The Story of American Architecture* (New York: W.W. Norton, 1936), next to page 224, for an early photograph. Ellis Wainwright, a collector of fine art, was more sensitive than Getty. Wainwright understood Sullivan's reasons for not including the Wainwright name on the tomb facade, and abided by Sullivan's design.
63. Sullivan, "Concerning the Imperial Hotel, Tokyo Japan" (Architectural Record, April 1923), 33, cited in Albert Bush-Brown, *Louis Sullivan* (New York: George Braziller, 1960), 6.
64. Sprague, 395, 402-403, and 409.

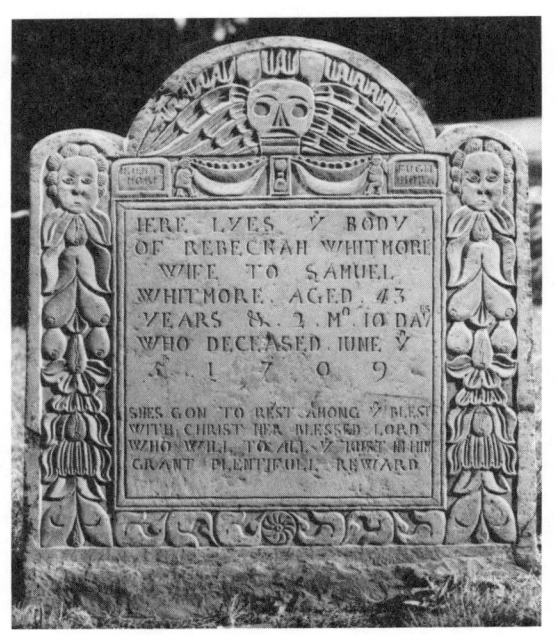

Figure 1. Rebeckah Whitmore, 1709, Lexington, MA, *Joseph Lamson*

Figure 2. Thankfull Foster, 1700, Dorchester, MA, *James Foster*

SEVEN INITIAL CARVERS OF BOSTON 1700-1725

Theodore Chase and Laurel K. Gabel

Boston and its environs in the opening decades of the eighteenth century was one of the most important gravestone carving centers of the New World. Joseph Lamson's shop in Charlestown was well established, providing markers for Boston as well as much of Middlesex County to the north and west (Fig. 1). James Foster and his son were supplying Dorchester and areas south and west with grave markers in their readily recognizable style (Fig. 2), and Boston's leading supplier of gravestones, master carver and mason William Mumford, was filling orders from his busy shop in the North End (Fig. 3). Although the combined output of these shops appears to have been prodigious, not a single signed or initialed gravestone has ever been found for these well established carvers.

In significant contrast, there are forty-three initialed stones attributed to seven young men who began carving in Boston during this same 1700-1725 period.[1] These men were: NL, Nathaniel Lamson (1692/3-1755); CL, Caleb Lamson (1697-1760); NE, Nathaniel Emmes (1690-1750); WG, William Grant (1694-1726); JG, James Gilchrist (1689-1722); WC, William Custin (?); and JN, John Noyes (1674-1749). These men and the stones bearing their initials have a number of characteristics in common:

a) All seven carvers worked in the Boston area within the same 1700-1725 time frame.
b) At least six of the seven were of approximately the same age. The initialed stones represent work done in their 'teens or early twenties, before they were established carvers and before any payments for their work appear in probate records.
c) The initialed stones are all slightly different - each stone is unique.
d) Most of the initialed examples are exceptionally well carved - "best efforts."
e) Many of the initialed stones are in coastal towns outside of the immediate Boston area: Marshfield, Marblehead, Salem, Duxbury, Barnstable, Quincy, Martha's Vineyard, MA, Portsmouth, NH, Norwalk, CT.
f) The initialed stones appear in a short time span of the carver's life, averaging about seven years (Fig. 4).

Figure 3. Ann Mumford, 1697/8, Newport, RI, *William Mumford*

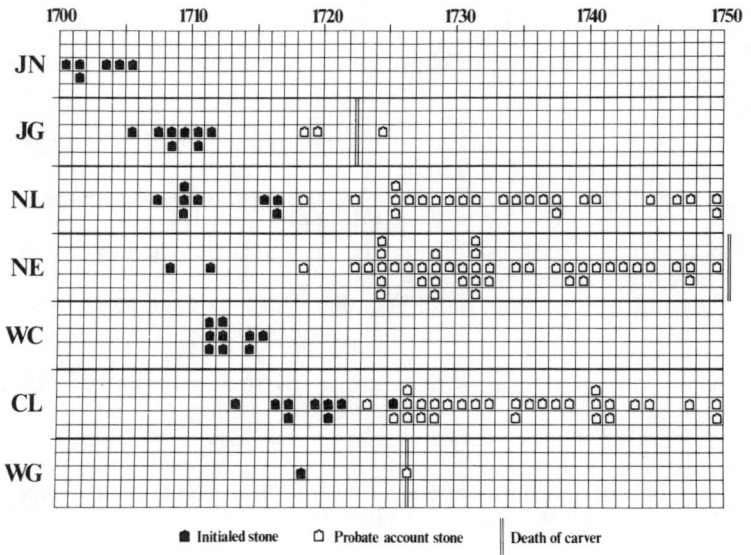

Figure 4. Chart of Seven Boston Initial Carvers

Joseph Lamson's sons, Nathaniel (1692/3-1755) and Caleb (1697-1760), almost certainly served as apprentices in their father's shop while still in their early 'teens. Naturally enough, most of their work bears the imprint of Joseph's training.

Nathaniel's eight initialed stones[2] span the years 1707-1716, when Nathaniel was between fifteen and twenty-four years of age. The workmanship is very accomplished. As with most of the other initialed stones, the carving often surpasses the standard workmanship of the carver's later years (Fig. 5).

Caleb Lamson's first initialed stone is dated 1713, shortly before Nathaniel's last one, and Caleb's initialed stones continue until 1725.[3] All but one were carved while Caleb was between the ages of sixteen and twenty-four (Fig. 6).

Figure 5. Capt. and Mrs. Pyam Blower, 1709, Cambridge, MA, *NL*

Figure 6. William Grimes, original date unknown - relettered stone, Lexington, MA, *CL*

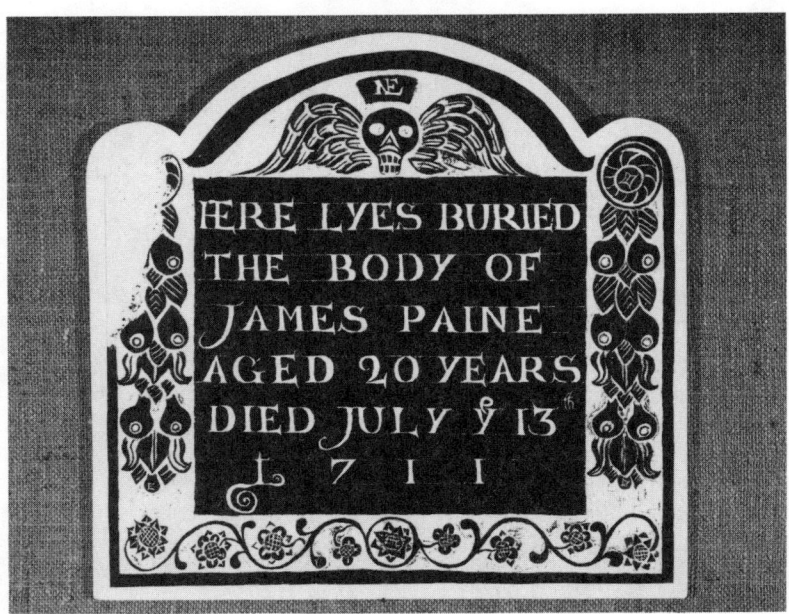

Figure 7. James Paine, 1711, Barnstable, MA, *NE*

If probate payments are any indication, one of Boston's most popular carvers in the first half of the eighteenth century was Nathaniel Emmes (1690-1750); payments to him are listed in more than eighty-five estates. But only two stones bearing his initials have been found[4] - both carved when Emmes was a very young man (Fig. 7). Later, however, as Harriette Merrifield Forbes suggests, he also cut his initials and the date March 31, 1729 on the cornerstone of the Old South Meeting House in Boston. Mrs. Forbes believes that Emmes lived on Prince Street in Boston's North End and learned the art of making gravestones from William Mumford.[5] The inventory in his estate shows a mansion house on Prince Street valued at L266-13-4.[6] Forbes calls both of his sons, Henry (1716-1767) and Joshua (1719-1772), stonecarvers. Henry did truly outstanding work, some of which, including a number of signed (not initialed) stones, are in Charleston, South Carolina.[7] As is true of all the initialed stones of other carvers, the stones initialed by Nathaniel Emmes appear several years before he begins to show up in probate accounts as a stonecarver paid for gravestones. Later in life, shortly before his death at the age of sixty, Nathaniel Emmes *signed* his name and location on the elegantly carved family crest medallion executed for John Dupuys, 1745, now in the vestry of Trinity Church in New York City. There is no question that in this case his full signature represents that of an artist signing his work.

The pair of stones for which William Grant (1694-1726) was paid in 1726 by the estate of Ambrose Vincent has not been found, making the WG initialed stone for Mary Marshall, 1718 Quincy, our only example of Grant's work (Fig. 8). The Marshall stone bears a lovely face with wings, much in the style of Gilchrist, Custin and Emmes, with whom Grant shared the carving market. Mrs. Forbes gives Grant's date of death as 1726, although there are some stones in his style carrying later dates. A carver named William Grant moved from Boston to New York about 1740. Whether this is the same or another William Grant, we do not know.[8]

Little has been learned or written about James Gilchrist (1689-1722), who during the ten or fifteen years before his early death shared the Boston carving market with others mentioned in this article (Fig. 9). Gilchrist was paid for gravestones in the estates of Stephen Butcher, Caleb Blanchard and

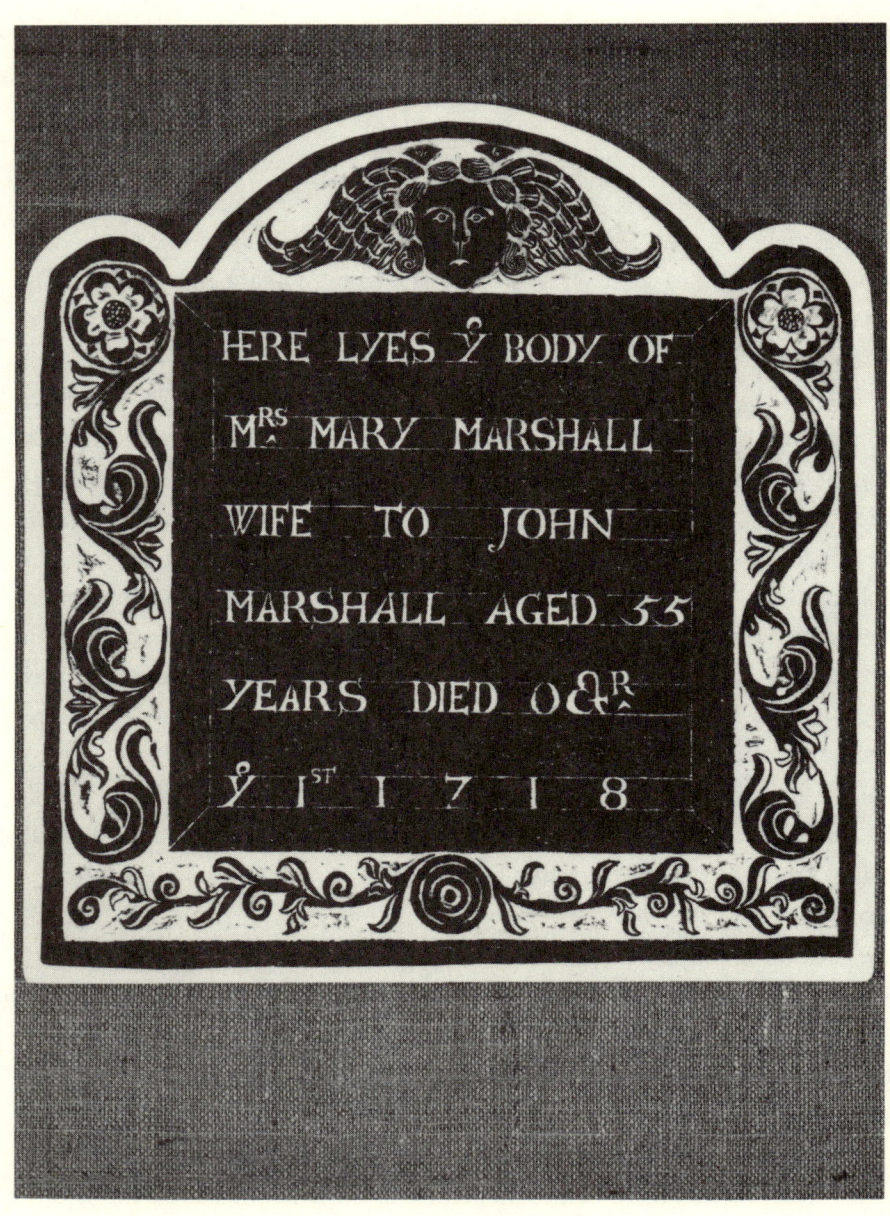

Figure 8. Mary Marshall, 1718, Quincy, MA, *WG*

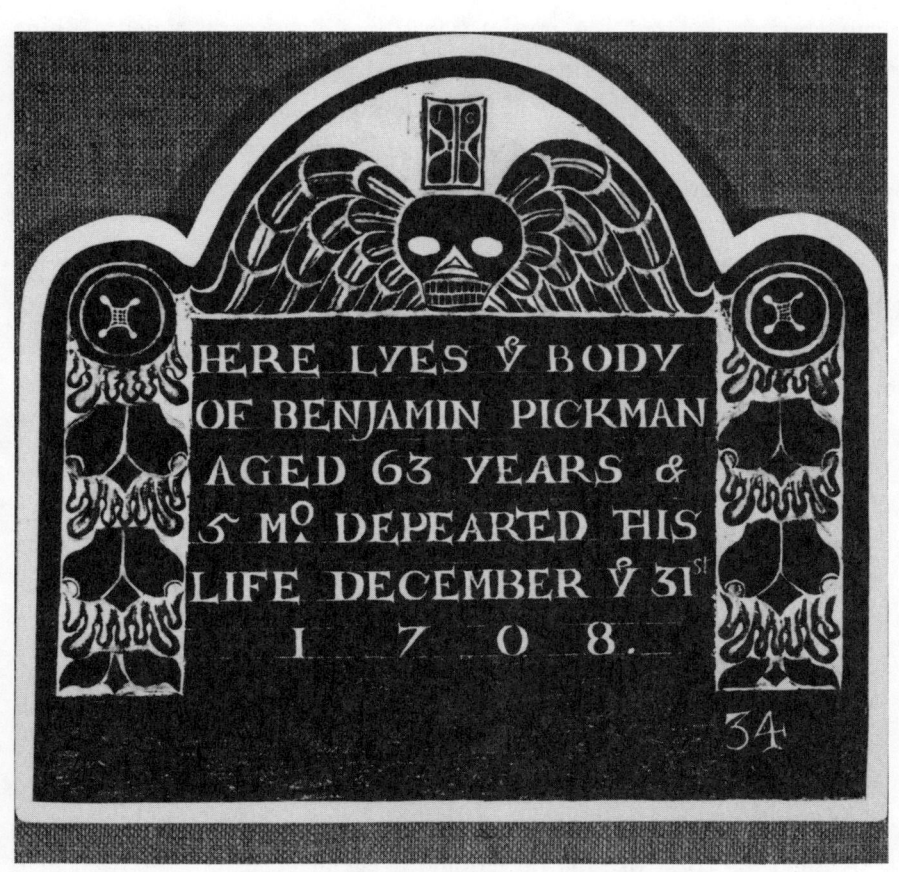

Figure 9. Benjamin Pickman, 1708, Salem, MA, *JG*

Samuel Tibbs, all of Boston.[9] None of these stones is still standing. The ledger of the New England Company, a missionary society known as the "Society for the Propagation of the Gospel in New England and the Parts Adjacent in America," contains a receipt dated 20 November 1718 for L6 paid to "James Gillkrist" for "fitting up" Samuel Sewall's tomb "in the new Burying place in Boston with wrought Connecticut stone, most of which I have already prepared." A receipt signed by Gilchrist and dated 18 June 1719 shows a further payment of L3 "in part due me." The tomb fitted up by Gilchrist was the Hull-Sewall family tomb in the Granary, and Sewall himself was buried there 7 January 1729/30. It still exists but does not serve as an example of Gilchrist's talent, having been relettered at some later date.[10]

Although there was a second JG (John Gaud) carving in Boston during this same 1700-1725 period, our study of this carver leads us to concur with Mrs. Forbes who believed that the stones initialed JG were probably the work of James Gilchrist. It appears that Gilchrist and Gaud were acquainted and may even have worked together, for there exists a record of their joint undertaking to fetch a load of slate from the islands in Boston Harbor.[11]

Kings' *Handbook of Boston Harbor*, although written 160 years after the events with which we are concerned, contains a vivid description of Slate Island, which may well have been the source of supply which James Gilchrist, John Gaud and other Boston carvers used:

> Slate Island, comprising about twelve acres and nearly nine and a half miles from Boston, is difficult of access except at high tide; when reached the aptness of the name is evident, for its slaty ledges run far out into the water, their black edges fringed by the light spray. The little beaches are covered by splinters and slabs of slate, which are ground and beaten to and fro by the waves, when they surge around these silent shores ... Around the coast rise the ragged and irregular edges of slate, well nigh concealed in places by a luxuriant growth of brown sea-weed and masses of kelp, which seem only floating upon the water's top, though they cling so closely to the rocks below, give the island an appearance as if hidden dangers were continually lurking around it ... On the north and west, towards Grape Island, are low gray cliffs of slate-rock, tier after tier, standing upon edge, or slanting backward or forward like ancient time-worn and weatherbeaten tombstones. Here schooners load with the slate; and one may see the quarries, all along, from which they have taken the material for countless cellar-walls and underpinnings.

The earliest stone bearing JG initials is a footstone for the Rev. Edward Tompson (1705) in the Winslow Burying Ground in Marshfield (Fig. 10). The Tompson headstone is clearly initialed JN, perhaps indicating some kind of working relationship between these two carvers (Fig. 11). James Gilchrist would have been about sixteen years old in 1705. The remaining seven stones initialed JG occur over the five-year period 1707-1711, when Gilchrist was between eighteen and twenty-two.[12] Like many other stonecutters of the period, Gilchrist very likely had a second trade. In an account in the estate of Abraham Adams, allowed in December 1717, Gilchrist is paid for carpentry.[13]

Figure 10. Rev. Edward Tompson footstone, 1705, Marshfield, MA (Forbes plate), *JN*

The Boston selectmen's records of 7 September 1714 show that the cellar under the northeast corner of the Town House rebuilt in 1711 (now the Old State House at the corner of State and Washington Streets) was rented at L9 per annum to James Gilchrist and a William Custin. Five months later, on 7 February 1715, the selectmen agreed that Gilchrist was to continue as tenant, and Custin was discharged from the lease.[14] These two entries suggest the intriguing possibility that the nine beautiful stones dated between 1711 and 1715 and initialed WC were carved by an associate of Gilchrist, William Custin (Figs. 12 and 13).[15]

The stone for Abigail Allen (1710) in West Tisbury bears the initials JG, and the stone for James Allen (1714), also in West Tisbury, the initials WC (Fig. 14). There are also two stones in Marblehead, one for Richard Gross (1711) and the other for Samuel Russell (1711) (Fig. 15), initialed WC and JG, respectively. This paired distribution lends further support for our belief that WC was James Gilchrist's associate, William Custin.

Figure 11. Rev. Edward Tompson headstone, 1705, Marshfield, MA, *JN*

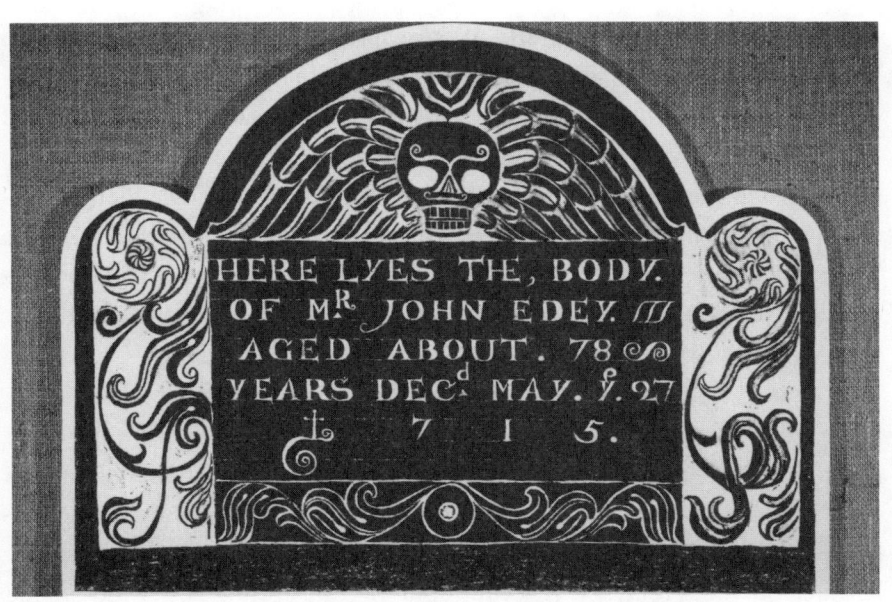

Figure 12. John Edey, 1715, West Tisbury, MA, *WC*

Figure 13. Mary Rickard, 1712, Plymouth, MA, *WC*

A search of the Massachusetts Archives provided us with an introduction to William Custin, for he there appears as a member of the successful expedition against Port Royal in 1710. This French post in Nova Scotia had long been a source of irritation to New England -- a center for attacks on its shipping and the scene of much illicit trading with New Englanders. Captured by Sir William Phips in 1690, it was returned to the French by the Treaty of Ryswick in 1697. An expedition from Boston in 1707 proved a disaster. Finally the British government took the matter in hand and sent forth a great fleet under Colonel Francis Nicholson consisting of five British men of war, the Massachusetts *Province Galley*, a hospital ship, some thirty troop ships and various smaller supporting vessels. 900 troops were recruited from Boston, 300 from Connecticut, 180 from Rhode Island and 100 from New Hampshire. The fleet set sail from Nantasket on 10 September 1710, Port Royal was taken, renamed Annapolis Royal and ceded to England in the Treaty of Utrecht. But one misfortune occurred in the operation. One of the transports was lost in attempting to pass through the narrow gut at the entrance of the Port Royal River. Nicholson describes the incident in his journal of the expedition:

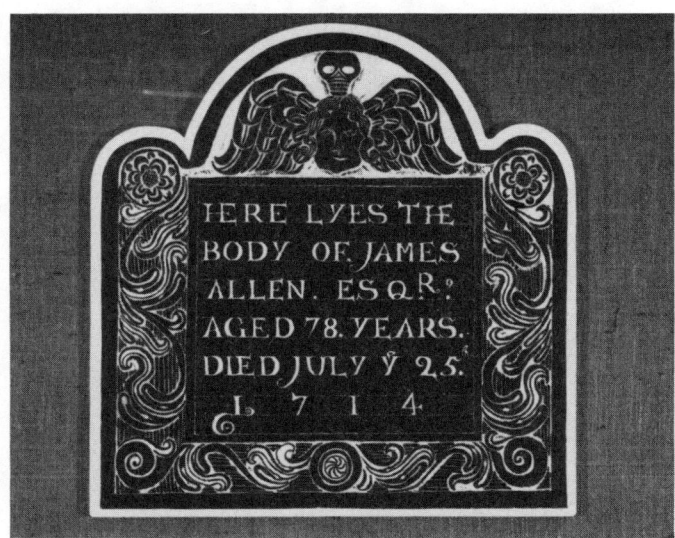

Figure 14. James Allen, 1714, West Tisbury, MA, *WC*

Figure 15. Samuel Russell, 1711, Marblehead, MA, *JG*

Capt Jeremiah Tay in the ship Caesar, assaying first to enter the River ran to near the Shoar as to ground his vessel, to whom help sufficient was tender'd, but he not being apprehensive of any danger, did not think fit to accept of it, and the wind rising with a violent swelling sea bulg'd the ship. In the evening; Lieut. Col. Ballantine and his Lieutenant with 7. more got into the Boat and with one paddle thro' great difficulty they got to Land, where the Boat bulg'd against the Rocks; Seventeen others of the Company swam to Land; 26 remaining on Board were drowned, vis. Capt. Tay, his Pilot or Sailor and 23. Souldiers.

William Custin was one of those who swam ashore. Another was Joseph Lamson, son of the Charlestown stonecutter. Ballantine and the survivors of his company took part in the action that followed and subsequently returned to Boston.[16]

We have found little further about Custin except a record of his marriage on 24 December 1714, just before his discharge from the shop lease, to Abigail Thayer, described only as "resident of Boston."[17] It is possible that Custin moved away from the Boston area after his marriage and the dissolution of his relations with Gilchrist. James Gilchrist retained the shop in the Boston Town House for three years and was then sued by the town treasurer for failure to pay the rent.[18]

On 30 September 1715 Gilchrist married Ann (Lambert) Shepcot. She had been married in 1713 to Sampson Shepcot, but her husband died only six weeks after the marriage. Ann was administratrix of Sampson's estate, and only three months before her remarriage she disposed of the "mansion house" at the foot of Water Street, next to Peter Oliver's Dock, which her first husband had inherited from his father, Thomas Shepcot, a prominent tobacconist. James Gilchrist and his wife Ann had a daughter Ann, born 15 September 1716. Gilchrist died 27 August 1722. His gravestone in the King's Chapel Burying Ground bears a winged skull and a bordered tympanum arch in the style of WC, John Gaud and Nathaniel Emmes (Fig. 16). Our current understanding of the work of these carvers leads us to favor WC or Emmes as the carver.[19]

Figure 16. James Gilchrist, 1722, Kings Chapel, Boston

Figure 17. Ichabod Wiswall, 1700, Duxbury, MA, *JN*

There are seven stones, all in Massachusetts, which bear the initials JN, six of which we can attribute to the carver JN (Fig. 17).[20] Like that of WC, JN's identity remains speculative. David Watters has developed a thesis, supported by persuasive circumstantial evidence, that JN was the Boston silversmith John Noyes (1674-1749).[21] Noyes was a member of the Brattle Street Church and of the Ancient and Honourable Artillery Company. Watters has collected a formidable list of JN's patrons who were connected in one way or another with John Noyes -- through purchases of his silver, as members of the Brattle Street Church, as members of the Artillery Company, or by connection with other silversmiths and pewterers. The Watters thesis is disputed by some experts on Colonial silver (Kathryn C. Buhler and Jonathan Fairbanks), who point out that John Noyes always signed his silver IN, while the gravestones are usually initialed JN, and who suggest that the delicate and precise work of a silversmith is incompatible with the tools and heavy hand required of a stonecarver. At the time the initials I and J were interchangeable, and in fact one of the JN stones, that of Martha Hall (1701) in Roxbury, bears the letters IN (Fig. 18).

Figure 18. Martha Hall, 1701, Roxbury, MA, *IN*

If JN was John Noyes, then he, unlike the other six initial carvers, did not initial stones when in his 'teens or early twenties, but in his late twenties and early thirties. There are no known payments for gravestones in Middlesex or Suffolk County probate records to anyone having the initials JN. John Noyes was definitely a silversmith at this time, for in 1700 the Benjamin Bachway estate paid him L5.8.4 for mourning rings. The same estate paid "William Mumford, the stonecutter's bill in full, L2.5.0," presumably for the grave marker (Suffolk Probate, 14:142). Mrs. Forbes lists in her notes on Suffolk probate records seven payments between 1709 and 1720 to John Nichols, some of them for funeral-related expenses such as making a coffin. Like Gilchrist, John Nichols was apparently a joiner or carpenter. Nichols was paid on at least one occasion for a coffin. Was he also a carver? Mrs. Forbes seems to have considered him as a possible JN. A review of Suffolk County probate accounts reveals instances where known stone carvers were paid for funeral related expenses other than gravestones. For example, in 1718 John Gaud was paid for bells, porters and cleaning the house, presumably for the funeral, while the same account shows a payment to William Mumford for the gravestones. Carver John Holms (Woodstock, CT, then part of Massachusetts) collected for "making two coffins and a gravestone." Nathaniel Emmes is paid for a coffin in 1736, and the Thomas Dakin estate in 1744 pays John Homer for a coffin and Nathaniel Emmes for the gravestone. Following her discussion of John Nichols, Mrs. Forbes asks whether William Dawes, the mason, was "The Stone Cutter of Boston." Records of the Third (Old South) Church suggest that a John Nichols, a member of that Church, was Dawes's son-in-law. This connection may not be significant but it opens another interesting line of inquiry. While we do not question the possibility that John Noyes, silversmith, was JN the gravestone carver, we do suggest that other possibilities exist and that further research may ultimately identify JN more positively.[22]

Comparison of the work of these seven initial carvers demonstrates a striking accord. With the possible exception of JN, the initialed stones represent the work of young apprentice or journeymen carvers before they have become established. Every initialed gravestone by these carvers is, with few exceptions, of a slightly different design. And the stones are, again with few exceptions, extremely well carved -- far more carefully executed and detailed than much of the carvers' later work. These facts suggest that the initialed stones may have been special projects or, like a young girl's needlework samplers, intended to demonstrate the carver's range of talent. In every case the initialed stones fall within a very brief time span, averaging less than seven years. The documented stones (i.e. those for which payments are shown in probate accounts) are found only after the initialed stones cease to appear. Roughly 75% of the initialed stones are outside of Boston and Charlestown, many of them far from this area. The pattern we have described -- the initialing of selected examples by gravestone cutters in the early stages of their career -- did not recur in later years in Boston, or, so far as we know, anywhere else. We can offer various explanations for this phenomenon.

The initialing does not seem to have been for advertising purposes: the initials are too discrete and obscure and would hardly serve to identify the carvers, particularly outside their home areas. However, if an apprentice worked in a shop or an area where there was more than one craftsman, initials would serve to identify his particular work. This could have been for the benefit of his employer. Or it could have been for his own benefit, either by way of recognition on the part of his employer of a particularly good piece of work or as a means of identifying something which the young man had done on his own time. Or perhaps each apprentice had to produce a certain number of stones -- from start to finish -- before being allowed to call himself a carver or before leaving the training program. Analogies may be found in other crafts. Thus a cabinet maker who has a number of apprentices may wish to identify the particularly good work of one of them by permitting him to initial it. The same practice, we are told, is known in the silversmith's craft, and may have prevailed in both crafts in the eighteenth century. William and Mary cane-seated chairs sometimes carry stamped or punched initials on the rear posts, indicating a division of labor resulting from piecework or jobbing out. Did a similar practice exist with stonecarvers?[23]

This at least seems clear: the practice of initialing selected work was adopted early in the eighteenth century and followed for a comparatively brief spell by Boston's young stonecarvers as they reached a point of perfection in their trade. Such a practice was not employed by mature carvers at work in the same period nor did these young carvers continue to initial stones after they themselves became established.

NOTES

1. These are listed in Sue Kelly and Anne Williams, "And the Men Who Made Them: The Signed Gravestones of New England," Journal of the Association of Gravestone Studies, *Markers II* (Lanham, MD, Univ. Press of America, 1983), 81, and the lists which follow in the footnotes to this article are taken therefrom. We are grateful to Sue Kelly and Anne Williams for permitting us to use reproductions of their admirable rubbings and to Daniel and Jessie Farber for providing all of the photographs of their work which appear in this article and for the photographs which appear in Figures 2 and 16. The photographs of the Pyam Blower headstone and of the Edward Thompson footstone (Figures 5 and 10) are from original glass plates made in the 1920s by Harriette Merrifield Forbes.
2. Stones initialed NL
    Samuel Blanchard, 1707, Andover, MA
    Rev. Jonathan Pierpont, 1709, Wakefield, MA
    Hannah & Mary Shutt, 1709, Boston
    Capt. & Mrs. Pyam Blower, 1709, Cambridge
    Mercy Oliver, 1710, Cambridge
    Mary Rous, 1715, Charlestown
    Thomas Sewall, 1716, Cambridge
    Ephraim Beach, 1716, Stratford, CT
3. Stones initialed CL
    Mary Reed, 1713, Marblehead
    Joseph Grimes, 1716, Stratford, CT (signed, not initialed)
    Prudence Turner, 1717, Marblehead
    John Mitchell, 1717, Malden
    John Rodgers, 1719, Portsmouth, NH
    Benjamin Allcock, 1720, Portsmouth, NH
    Joseph Small, 1720, Portsmouth, NH
    Richard & Lydia Webber, 1721, Portsmouth, NH
    Margaret Gardner, 1725, Portsmouth, NH

    The stone now marking the grave of William Grimes, 1766, Lexington, MA bears the Lamson carving style and the initials "CL." It is not possible to date the stone since the original tablet carving has been smoothed down and recarved. It is not included in our survey.
4. Stones initialed NE
    Arthur Mason, 1708, Boston
    James Paine, 1711, Barnstable
5. Harriette Merrifield Forbes, *Gravestones of Early New England and the Men Who Made Them 1653-1800*, (Boston: Houghton Mifflin, 1927; reprint, New York; De Capo Press, 1967), 57-58.
6. Suffolk Probate No. 9495.
7. Diana Williams Combs, *Early Gravestone Art in Georgia and South Carolina* (Athens, GA:

University of Georgia Press, 1986).
8. Estate of Ambrose Vincent, Suffolk Probate, Bk. 24, p. 539. Richard F. Welch, *Memento Mori: The Gravestones of Early Long Island 1680-1810* (Syosset, N.Y. Friends for Long Island's Heritage, 1983), 51-52.
9. Suffolk Probate No. 3682, Bk. 21 p. 82; No. 4074, Bk. 21 p. 382; No. 3666, Bk. 23 p. 449.
10. George Parker Winship, "Samuel Sewall and the New England Company, MHS *Proceedings*, 2d. Ser. 67:88. The original ledger is at the Massachusetts Historical Society, S. Sewall Coll., see p. 83 and see *Diary of Samuel Sewall*, ed. M. Halsey Thomas, 2 vols. (New York: Farrar, Strauss and Giroux, 1973), 1:415n. Sewall was active in the work of the New England Company and held the post of Commissioner's secretary 1700-1724 and treasurer 1701-1724. Sewall's first wife, Hannah Hull, died 19 October 1719, and a diary entry for 16 September 1721 (after the death of his second wife) reads: "I set up my Connecticut stone post in the Elm pasture, in Remembrance of my loving wife Mrs. Hannah Sewall." *Diary of Samuel Sewall*, 1:xxvii, xxviii; 2:982. For reference to Deane's Pasture (which Sewall called Elm Pasture), at the west end of the Common, see entry for 8 May 1685, *Diary*, 1:62, and also the earlier edition of the Diary appearing in the MHS *Collections*, 5th Ser. 5:73n and Annie Haven Thwing, *The Crooked & Narrow Streets of the Town of Boston 1630 - 1822* (Boston, Charles E. Lauriat Co., 1930), 168.
11. Forbes, 56. Theodore Chase and Laurel K. Gabel, "John Gaud: Boston and Connecticut Gravestone Carver 1693-1750," *The Connecticut Historical Society Bulletin*, (No.2, 1985) 50:76.
12. Stones initialed JG
    Rev. Edward Tompson, 1705, Marshfield
    Zacheus Barton, 1707, Salem
    Thomas Kellon, 1708, Boston
    Benjamin Pickman, 1708, Salem
    Mary Green, 1709, Boston
    Lt. John Mackintosh, 1710, Boston
    Abigail Allen, 1710, Martha's Vineyard
    Samuel Russell, 1711, Marblehead
13. Suffolk Probate No. 2568, Bk. 20, p. 150.
14. *Reports of the Record Commissioners of the City of Boston*, 39 vols. (Boston, 1881-1909), 11:215, 240.
15. Stones initialed WC
    Elizabeth Sande (1711), Old Burial Hill, Marblehead
    Richard Gross (1711), Old Burial Hill, Marblehead
    Thomas Lanyon (1711), Granary
    Mary Rickard (1712), Old Buryal Hill, Plymouth
    Joseph Phippene (1712), Fairfield, CT
    William Hanes (1712), East Norwalk Historical Cemetery, East Norwalk, CT
    William Thomas (1714), Old Burial Hill, Plymouth
    James Allen (1714), West Tisbury
    John Edey (1715), West Tisbury
16. Massachusetts Archives, 71:755. Francis Nicholson's Journal, *Boston Newsletter*, 30 October and 6 November, 1710 and *Nova Scotia Historical Society Collections* (Halifax, 1879), 1:65-66. See also Thomas Hutchinson, *The History of the Colony and Province of Massachusetts-Bay*. Lawrence Shaw Mayo, ed. (Cambridge, Harv. Univ. Press, 1936), 2:134-137; Samuel Penhallow, *A History of the Wars of New England*, (Boston:1726), 52-56; Samuel Niles, "A Summary Historical Narrative of the Wars in New England", Mass. Hist. Soc. *Collections* (Fourth Series) 5:311.321; and George A. Rawlyk, *Nova Scotia's Massachusetts - A Study of Massachusetts-Nova Scotia Relations 1630-1784* (Montreal and

London: McGill-Queen's Univ. Press, 1973), 117-123. As to Joseph Lamson see William J. Lamson, *Descendants of William Lamson of Ipswich, Mass. 1634-1917*, (New York: Tobias A. Wright, 1917), 28, 42; Mary E. Donahue, *Massachusetts Officers and Soldiers 1702-1722: Queen Anne's War to Drummers War* (Boston: New England Historic Genealogical Society, 1980). And as to Ballantine see Clifford K. Shipton, *Sibley's Harvard Graduates* (Cambridge: Harv. Univ. Press, 1933), 4:198, especially as to the wardrobe and extensive provisions he lost in the wreck of the *Caesar*.

17. *Boston Marriages 1700-1809*, 2 vols. (Baltimore: Genealogical Publishing Co., 1977, based on *Reports of the Record Commissioners*, vols. 28 and 29), 1:94.

18. Suffolk County Court Records, Massachusetts Archives, No. 14993.

19. Ann's marriages: *Boston Marriages* 1:47, 58. Sampson Shepcot's estate: Suffolk Probate No. 3530; 18:210, 244; N.S. 7:305,307. Deed of the mansion: Suffolk Deeds, 29:221. Birth of daughter: *Boston Births* 2:114. Gilchrist's death: Gilchrist's gravestone describes him as having died in his thirty-fourth year, and if this is to be taken as reliable evidence, then he was born in 1689 and not 1687 as indicated in Mrs. Forbes's list and in subsequent lists of New England stonecutters. For more about Thomas Shepcot (Shapcott, Shapcoat, Shepcott, etc.) see *Reports of the Record Commissioners of the City of Boston* 39 vols. (Boston, 1881-1909) 1:54,122,156; 7:127,183,215; Suffolk Deeds, 9:285; Suffolk Probate, No. 2817; 15:172. Sampson was a shipwright, one brother-in-law, William Butler, was a shipwright, another, Jonathan Allen, was a joiner, and it is possible that James Gilchrist as a carpenter was at some time associated with them.

In his will Thomas left his son Sampson "(if in the Judgment of Sober, honest and Judicious Neighbors his Master being one he shall well, orderly and soberly bear and behave himself, and be a good husband then in such case and no otherwise) L100 to be paid at 21 and also all my dwelling house, land and wharfe thereunto belonging and adjoining, with the right of [his daughters] Martha and Mary to live in half the house as long as they are unmarried without any trouble, disturbance, interruption, ejection or molestation whatsoever from their brother Sampson...But if (according to the judgment aforesaid) Sampson shall prove an ill husband and lead a lewd, vicious and disorderly life, then he is to receive L10 and no more, and the real estate is to be divided between Mary and Martha."

Shortly after the death of James Gilchrist, on 11 March 1722/3, his widow filed some sort of petition with the selectmen, but no further record of it appears. *Reports of the Record Commissioners*, 8:171. An Ann Gilchrist, described as "single woman" and "spinster" in the probate papers, died in 1743 and left a nuncupative will, that is, oral instructions given to witnesses:

"Ann Gilcrest of Boston, single woman, being in the house of Lydia Lewis, widow, sick and nearing her end, bid her nurse to fetch two bonds and deliver them to Mrs. Lewis, and Mrs. Lewis to take all she had and give the remainder to her kinswoman Susy (whom we believe to be Susannah Hyley)."

Ann left tangibles valued at L130-13-8, cash of L210-9-7 and a note for L6. This may have been James Gilchrist's daughter Ann. Suffolk Probate No. 7904; 36:324,527-529.

20. Stones initialed JN

Ichabod Wiswall, 1700, Duxbury
Sarah Dolbeare, 1701, Copps Hill, Boston
Martha Hall, 1701, Roxbury
John Cleverly, 1703, Quincy
Mehitabel Hammond, 1704, Newton
Edward Thompson, 1705, Marshfield
John Woodcock, 1718, Dedham

The John Woodcock stone in Dedham listed by Kelly and Williams is almost certainly by John Gaud; the initials scratched on the brow of the skull may stand for John the Carver

or John the deceased.
21. David Watters, "The JN Carver", *Markers II*, 115.
22. Mrs. Forbes's notes are at the American Antiquarian Society. The payments to Nichols appear in Suffolk Probate Bk. 17, p. 26; Bk. 18, p. 67; Bk. 19, p. 172; Bk. 21, p. 611; Bk. 9, p. 17; Bk. 21, p. 711; and Bk. 18, p. 432. The payments to Gaud and Mumford in estate of Hannah Hendley, Suffolk Probate, Bk. 20, p. 447; the payment to John Holms in estate of Joseph Bartholemew, Suffolk Probate, Bk. 24, p. 25; the payment to Nathaniel Emmes for a coffin in estate of Alexander Sears, Suffolk Probate, Bk. 33, p. 14; and the payments to Homer and Emmes in the estate of Thomas Dakin are found in Suffolk Probate, Bk. 37, p. 80. As to the Dawes family see *Historical Catalogue of the Old South Church (Third Church) Boston* (Boston: 1883), 226, 232, 281, 285, 287, 324; and see will of Ambrose Dawes (son of William), Suffolk Probate No. 2987, referring to "my Brother Mr. John Nicholls."
23. We are indebted to Jonathan L. Fairbanks, Curator of American Decorative Arts at the Boston Museum of Fine Arts, and Robert B. St. George, a professor of American studies at Boston University, for the information contained in this paragraph.

Contributors

Jessie Lie Farber was a founder of the Association for Gravestone Studies, a former editor of its *Newsletter* and editor of Markers I. Her husband Daniel Farber is an eminent photographer, and his work appears in many books and articles on gravestones.

Laurel K. Gabel and Theodore Chase are members of the Association for Gravestone Studies and former officers. Mrs. Gabel is a member of the Friends of Mt. Hope Cemetery in Rochester, New York. Mr. Chase is president of the New England Historic Genealogical Society and a member of the Council of the Massachusetts Historical Society.

Thomas E. Graves holds a doctorate in folklore and folklife from the University of Pennsylvania. He has taught at The Pennsylvania State University - Capitol Campus and at Ursinus College. The thrust of his research continues to be arts and belief systems of the Pennsylvania Germans.

Darrell A. Norris is Associate Professor of Geography at the State University of New York College at Geneseo, where he has taught since 1981. Professor Norris earned his Ph.D. at McMaster University, Hamilton, Ontario, where he completed his research project on Ontario cemeteries and was Research Associate for the second volume of the forthcoming Historical Atlas of Canada. He is also Director of Geneseo's Developmental Impact Studies Center, a research unit devoted to community-based economic, social, and demographic analysis.

Deborah Trask is editor of the Association's *Newsletter*. She is the Assistant Curator, History Section, Nova Scotia Museum in Halifax, Nova Scotia. Debra McNabb has her MA in geography from the University of British Columbia and is Research Data Coordinator for the Canadian Museum of Civilization in Ottawa.

Meredith Williams is a 1986 graduate of Yale, where she majored in art history. She now teaches English and studies Japanese in Tokyo. Her father, Gray Williams, is a freelance writer on subjects ranging from history to science.

Robert A. Wright graduated from Kenyon College with a degree in studio art. Further studies at the Visual Studies Workshop in Rochester, NY broadened his photographic education. He is a freelance photographer and writer, residing in Madison, WI.

Index of Carvers, and of Illustrated Gravestones and their Location

Allen, James, 222
Atwater, Lydie, 47

Baldwin, Michael, 3, 5, 6, 7, 8, 11, 13, 14, 15, 32, 36, 37, 41, 55
Barnstable, 214
Beard, Ruth, 23
Beecher, Thomas, 34
Bernville, 87
Bethel, 8, 37
Blainsport, 104
Blower, Capt. and Mrs. Pyam, 213
Blumbauer, Philip, 118
Bngl, Johan, 104
Boffenmoyer, Samuel, 87
Bradley, Mary, 35
Branford, 17
Brickerville, 103, 106, 113
Brooklyn, New York, 29
Brooks, John, 9

Cambridge, 213
Carrington, Elias, 49
Chestnut Level, Lancaster County, 98, 103, 108, 112
Chipman's Corner, 159
Clark, John, 108
Collins, Benjamin, 153
Cook, Eunice, 42
Cromirin, Catrina, 111
Cunningham, James, 119
Curtis, Hulda and infant daughter, 9
Custin, William, 211, 220, 222, 223
Cutler, Jonathan, 48

Davis, Eliakim, 8
Dawes, William, 227
Derby, 23, 28
Derby Carver, 23, 24, 29, 30, 31, 47, 55
Dorchester, 210
Douglas, Benjamin, 19
Duxbury, 225

East Greenville, 108
East Haven, 18
Edey, John, 221

Eichelberger, Salome, 107
Emmes, Henry, 215
Emmes, Joshua, 215
Emmes, Nathaniel, 211, 215, 224, 227
Ephrata, 69, 109, 114
Erb, Mariah, 81

Fairfield, CT, 11, 32
Fairfield, PA, 98, 121
Fitch, Rachel, 158
Foster, James, 211
Foster, Thankfull, 210
Freyen, H., 114

Gaud, John, 218, 224, 227
Getty Tomb, 180
Gilbert, James, 45, 46
Gilbert, Mary, 33
Gilbert, Rebecca, 33
Gilchrist, James, 211, 215, 218, 219, 220, 223, 224, 227
Gold, Hezekiah, 42
Gold, Thomas, 1, 52, 56
Grant, William, 211, 215
Griffin, James C. & Thomas, 156
Grimes, William, 214

Hall, Martha, 226
Hanover, 107
Harris, Eunice, 155
Hawley, Edward, 22
Hellertown, 99
Herb, Andreas, 64
Hickock, Ebenezer, 37
Hill Church, Berks County, 60, 64, 71, 81
Holms, John, 227
Homer, John, 227
Hotchkiss, Caleb, 2
Howell, John, 16
Howell, Mary, 16
Huffs Church, Berks County, 118
Hull, Joseph, 28

Ives, Mariah, 50
Ives, Sally, 50

Judson, Abner, 7
Judson, Agur, 40
Junt, George, 109

KD, 108
Keller, Elisabeth, 69
Kentville, 155, 156
Kings Chapel, Boston, 224
Kunsin, Elisabet, 100

Lamson, Caleb, 211, 213
Lamson, Joseph, 211
Lamson, Nathaniel, 211, 213
Lang, Peter, 79
Laubenbach, C., 86
Lautenbach, C.H., 79, 85
Leonhard Miller, 106
Lexington, 210, 214
Littlestown, 100
Lower Saucon Township, near Hellertown, 117

Madison, 48
Magee, Henry, 156
Manning family, 153
Marblehead, 223
Marshall, Mary, 216
Marshfield, 219, 220
Matz, Lydia, 85
Mehetabel, 50
Meigs, Chloe, 48
Menich, James R., 119
Meriden, 26
Merwin, Mary, 38
Midlto, John, 98
Miles, Martha, 44
Miles, Susannah, 30
Milford, 13, 30, 38, 43, 44, 49
Miller, John, 12
Millerin, Anna, 103
Millroie, Thomas, 103
Miner, Thomas, 158
Mumford, Ann, 212
Mumford, William, 211, 227

New Haven, 2, 12, 16, 19, 20, 33, 37, 45, 47, 48, 50
Newport, 212
Newton, Amadeus, 51
Nichols, John, 227
Northford, 27

Noyes, John, 211, 225, 227

Oberle, Rudolph, 99
Oberly, Rudolf, 117
Orwigsburg, 79, 85

Paine, James, 214
Parmele, Elias, 20
Peck, Benjamin, 155
Penryn, 111
Perkins, David, 19
Peterman, Daniel, 65
Pickman, Benjamin, 217
Plymouth, 221
Pond, Martha, 43
Prudden, Job, 13

Quincy, 216

Redding, 21
Reynold, Samuel, 98
Rice, Mindwell, 26
Rickard, Mary, 221
Ritter, David, 3, 46, 47, 49, 51, 53, 55, 57
Roxbury, 226
Royce, Elizabeth, 26
Russell, Samuel, 223
Ryerson Tomb, 168

Salem, 217
Sanford, Daniel and Jeremiah, 21
Seaman, Abraham, 154, 157, 160, 161, 162, 163
Second Horton Carver, 154, 157, 162
Seipel, Susan, 66
Shelton, 40
Sherman, Ebenezer, 35
Sigmund, Friedrich, 118
Silliman, Ebenezer, 11
Sinclair, Elizabeth, 2
Steel, Elisabeth, 112
Stoothoff, Wilhelmus, 29
Stratford, 7, 9, 10, 14, 18, 22, 23, 35, 42
Sullivan gravestone, 203
Sullivan, Louis Henri, 169

Thompson, Lydia, 33
Tomlinson, Agur, 18

Tomlinson, Mary Alice, 10
Tomlinson, Rebeckah, 14
Tompson, Rev. Edward, 219, 220
Trexlertown, 66

Upper Canard, 155

Wainwright Tomb, 194
Wallingford, 26
Waugh, Jane, 121
Weidman, Elizabeth, 113
West Tisbury, 221, 222
Whitmore, Rebeckah, 210
Willcockson, Samuel, 23
Willford, Elisabeth, 17
Williams, Anne, 27
Wiswall, Ichabod, 225
Wolfville, 158
Woodbridge, 19, 34, 35, 42, 51
Woodward, Huldah, 18
Woodworth, Ezekiel, 159
Wyatt, Alice, 32

Yoder, Abraham, 71

Review Requested:
We'd like to know if you enjoyed the book. Please consider leaving a review on the platform from which you purchased the book.

CPSIA information can be obtained
at www.ICGtesting.com
Printed in the USA
LVHW111331180720
661048LV00002B/400